3

THE TOBACCO INDUSTRY IN THE UNITED STATES

STUDIES IN HISTORY, ECONOMICS AND PUBLIC LAW

EDITED BY THE FACULTY OF POLITICAL SCIENCE OF
COLUMBIA UNIVERSITY

Volume XXVI] [Number 3

THE TOBACCO INDUSTRY IN THE UNITED STATES

BY

MEYER JACOBSTEIN

AMS PRESS
NEW YORK

COLUMBIA UNIVERSITY
STUDIES IN THE
SOCIAL SCIENCES

70

The Series was formerly known as *Studies in History, Economics and Public Law.*

Reprinted with the permission of Columbia University Press
From the edition of 1907, New York
First AMS EDITION published 1968
Manufactured in the United States of America

Library of Congress Catalogue Card Number: 68-56662

AMS PRESS, INC.
New York, N.Y. 10003

PREFACE

So far as the writer is aware, no broad and comprehensive study of the tobacco industry in this country has ever been made. The technical and statistical report in the United States census of 1880 is now antiquated. Mr. B. W. Arnold's investigation of the industry in Virginia covers only a small fraction of the whole field, and that only for a short period.[1] The best work on the technical aspect of the industry was written by Killibrew and Myrick.[2] What is lacking is a general study of the historical development of the industry as a whole, and an analysis of some of the special internal problems, of interest not merely to the planter or the manufacturer but to the economist and economic historian.

In view of the great influence of the tobacco industry on our colonial development, as well as the magnitude of the industry to-day, no apology need be offered for such a study. Up to the close of the eighteenth century tobacco was the chief commercial crop of the South, and was the second in importance of all our exports. Our country has remained to this day the largest tobacco-growing country in the world. We supply not only ourselves with the leaf, but European markets as well. No small part of

[1] Published as a dissertation in Johns Hopkins University *Studies in Historical and Political Science*, vol. xv, 1897.

[2] *Tobacco Leaf*, by J. B. Killibrew and Herbert Myrick, 1903, published by Orange Judd Company. It is a hand-book of methods of cultivation, curing, packing, etc.

our national economic energy is employed in this industry. To trace its development from the earliest Virginia plantation to the modern gigantic Trust is one of the aims of this investigation and research.

The writer, however, has not confined himself to a mere study in economic history. The continuity and evolutionary development of the industry are regarded only in so far as they do not sacrifice his second purpose, namely, to present, in an intensive way, an analysis of the interesting features of the organization of the industry as it exists to-day. In pursuing this second purpose, the study should appeal most to those economists who are interested in the actual structure and organization of our industrial society as we see it and live in it to-day. Looked at in this light, it is a study of a typical unit or atom of a larger system, and hence may serve as a concrete contribution to an inductive economics.

The author is indebted to Mr. G. W. Perkins, E. Lewis Evans, and H. W. Riley for kindly supplying him with information concerning labor unions in the tobacco industry. To Mr. M. W. Diffly he is grateful for the material furnished concerning the problems of the retailer. For some important data regarding the economic conditions of the Southern planter the author is gratefully indebted to Mr. L. S. Thomas, Martinsville, Va. But the writer is under special obligation to Professors E. R. A. Seligman, H. R. Seager and H. L. Moore for their valuable criticisms and suggestions while the dissertation was in progress, as well as for their assistance in revising the manuscript and the proof.

MEYER JACOBSTEIN.

COLUMBIA UNIVERSITY, *May*, 1907.

CONTENTS

PART I—HISTORICAL SURVEY

CHAPTER I

The Colonial Period

CHAPTER II

1776–1860

PAGE

PART II—MODERN PERIOD (1860-1905)

CHAPTER I

Consumption

CHAPTER II

Cultivation: Agrarian Problems

CHAPTER III

Manufacture

CHAPTER IV

The Tobacco Trust

PAGE

CHAPTER V

Labor Conditions in the Tobacco Industry

CHAPTER VI

Foreign Trade

CHAPTER VII

The Tobacco Tax

CHAPTER VIII

PART I.—HISTORICAL SURVEY

CHAPTER I

The Colonial Period

Into the antiquities of tobacco, its origin and religious significance, it is not our purpose to enter. Our story begins with its introduction into Europe as a commercial crop, about the middle of the sixteenth century.[1] Spanish merchants brought it into Europe from the West Indies. A European market for tobacco had therefore existed for about fifty years before permanent English settlements were made in America. At the opening of the seventeenth century its sale in England was large enough to arouse anxiety among the Bullionists, who hated to see the precious metals leaving the country in exchange for a "worthless weed." In order to check its consumption, Parliament increased the import tax on tobacco from two pence to six shillings ten pence per pound.[2] That the tobacco trade had gained some importance at this early date may be inferred from the fact that by 1601 some individuals thought it worth while to buy a monopoly on the manufacture and sale of tobacco pipes.[3] It remained for the American colonists

[1] It is reported that tobacco was first brought into Europe via Portugal by Spanish merchants in the year 1558. Jean Nicot, the French minister at Lisbon, introduced the commodity into France.

[2] Hazard's *Collection*, pp. 49-50.

[3] *Parliamentary History, 43 Elizabeth*, 1601.

to take advantage of the existing market and develop it still further.

Fortunately for the colonists, there were economic and political forces at work abroad coöperating with their own efforts to capture and develop the market. England's practical commercial policy laid emphasis on the necessity of having a favorable balance of trade, in order to prevent too much bullion from flowing out of the country. The House of Commons voted unanimously (1620) "that the importation of Spanish tobacco is one of the causes of want of money within the kingdom." [1] Therefore, when it was learned that tobacco could be grown in the Anglo-American colonies, Parliament [2] decided to cut off the importation of Spanish tobacco, which, in 1621, amounted to £60,000. In 1621 Parliament enacted a law practically prohibiting the importation of foreign tobacco by levying discriminating duties in favor of colonial tobacco and against all foreign tobacco. This preferential tariff remained in vogue during the entire colonial period, and was one important factor in the building up of the tobacco industry on this continent.

A second cause operating in favor of the American colonies was the general English colonial policy, which had as one of its aims the development of colonial natural resources, while at the same time, creating a colonial market for the home manufactures in the colonies.

[1] 13th March, 18 James I.

[2] *Parliamentary History*, pp. 1196, 1197; 19 James I. Mr. Edwin Sandys, arguing the case of the Bullionists, figured that England really lost £120,000 through importation of Spanish tobacco. For, he argued, not only did £60,000 go out of the kingdom but that £60,000 would come into the kingdom, if the colonies raised the tobacco, from the sale of the latter in European markets.

While closely akin to the Bullionist policy, the Colonial program was quite distinct, and operated long after the former was discarded. Speaking of the discriminating duty on foreign tobacco, Chalmers says, this is "the first instance of the modern policy of promoting the importation of the commodities of the colonies in preference to the production of foreign nations."[1] This policy was further re-enforced by prohibiting the cultivation of tobacco in the home country and in Ireland.[2] In 1652, for instance, we find the following significant passage: "Whereas divers great quantities of tobacco have been of late years and now are planted in divers parts of this nation tending to the decay of husbandry and tillage, the prejudice and hindrance of the English plantations abroad and the trading and commerce and navigation and shipping of this nation" and so forth.[3] Therefore a penalty was laid upon home cultivation of tobacco. The chief tobacco-growing counties of England, Gloucestershire and Worcester, offered resistance to this prohibition but finally gave in. Though no great sacrifice was entailed, since England's soil was not adapted to tobacco culture, the mere existence of the statutes indicates the consistency with which English statesmen pushed this colonial policy. Later developments of the tobacco trade fully justified England's policy, for she not only was able to import from her American colonies sufficient tobacco for home consump-

[1] Chalmer's *Annals*, p. 51.

[2] 12 Chas. II, c. 34; also 22–23 Chas. II, c. 26.

[3] Prohibited by 12 Charles II, c. 34 and 15 Charles II, c. 7. Same prohibition extended to Ireland in 1660, and to Scotland by act of 22 Geo. III, c. 73. Ireland was again granted permission to grow tobacco in 1779, but lost that privilege again in 1831 (1 and 2 William IV, c. 13). There are still restrictions to-day on its cultivation in Ireland.

tion, but profited greatly by supplying Europe with her surplus.

Nor was the King himself disinterested in the expansion of the tobacco trade. For in spite of his "Counterblaste" against the use of tobacco, King James I was not opposed to increasing his income by the sale of a monopoly in the trading of tobacco. Under the pretense that a monopoly enjoyed by a few individuals would check the consumption of tobacco, the King was able to harmonize his moral repulsion to tobacco with personal financial gain. In 1621 the patent yielded James I annually as much as £16,000.[1] Out of deference to a protest from Virginia planters against the abuse of the Tobacco Monopoly, the patent was withdrawn in 1621, but again farmed out in 1625.[2] The farmers of the customs demanded a tax of one shilling on each pound of tobacco imported into England. The colonists denounced this as a violation of their charter rights, which provided for a tax of only five per cent on all imported goods, and maintained that the monopoly granted to the "Farmers of Revenue" was equivalent to an additional and illegal tax. The Virginia Company fought so stubbornly against the monopoly that the King yielded and finally withdrew all monopoly rights from the "Farmers of Revenue."[3]

If it was to the King's interest to have the tobacco trade grow, since the value of the monopoly privilege varied directly with the extent of the business done, all the more so was it to the interest of the Virginia Company to encourage it. The financial success of these

[1] 19 James I, 1621.

[2] Hazard's *Collection*, pp. 224-225; also Chalmers' *Annals*, p. 128.

[3] *Cf.* Chalmer's *Annals*, p. 46, for struggle between the Virginia Company and the "Farmers of Revenue."

colonizing companies depended upon the development of the natural resources. In the first charter of Virginia (1606) the London Company was allowed to impose a tax of two and one-half per cent. and five per cent. on all goods "trafficked bought or sold" by English citizens or foreigners respectively. It was by no mere coincidence that the Virginia Company was always back of legislation that shut out foreign goods from England's market whenever Virginia's products could be substituted. Mr. Sandys, who was instrumental in pushing through this legislation, especially the prohibitory act of 1624, was the first treasurer of the Virginia Company. Economic self-interest reflected itself there as it does now in governmental policy. Prosperity in Virginia meant a greater demand for land, and a corresponding increase in quit-rents for the individual stockholders of the company. No small part of the company's profits came from trading, which in turn increased with the development of tobacco cultivation. Hence the Virginia Company was also a factor in the upbuilding of this industry in America.

Thus far, we have spoken only of what might be termed the external conditions that favored the cultivation of tobacco in the American colonies: first, the national financial policy, or Bullionist theory, desiring to check the exportation of bullion by prohibiting the importation of Spanish tobacco, thus creating a home market for colonial tobacco; second, the general colonial policy of encouraging the importation of raw material from the colonies, and exporting to them finished products, while at the same time, increasing the carrying trade for English ships; third, the increase in the King's revenues through the sale of tobacco monopolies; and fourth, the interest of the Virginia Company in booming land values, as well as in the direct profits resulting from the trade that was formerly in the hands of Spanish merchants who brought tobacco from the West Indies. All these forces combined to give the first impetus to tobacco cultivation in the American colonies.

We turn now to the more fundamental, internal causes, without which the above encouragements would have been in vain. First, and most essential, comes the soil. Southern soil was rich, fertile and plentiful, and favorably situated for tobacco cultivation. Flat river land with its rich, black mould was just the kind needed for this crop. And the situation of vast stretches of this fertile land along navigable streams in Virginia and Maryland, eliminated the expenses of inland transportation, which in those days were very heavy. Concerning the adaptability of the soil for tobacco, we have Captain John Smith's testimony before the Royal Commission; when asked why Virginia did not grow wheat instead of tobacco, he replied that a man's labor in tobacco cultivation was worth six times that in raising wheat. In his day wheat sold for two shillings six pence per bushel, tobacco for three shillings per pound, or, in terms of labor value, £10 for grain, £60 for tobacco, a ratio of 1 : 6 in favor of tobacco. One reason for the relative profitableness of tobacco culture was this: wheat was more of an extensive crop, requiring greater area than tobacco, which was always, relative to wheat, an intensive crop. To clear land in those days was an expensive undertaking, especially before slave labor was utilized. Fresh and newly-cleared land was highly productive for tobacco, and so we find that only the abandoned tobacco fields were given up to wheat or corn cultivation.[1] Cot-

[1] *American Husbandry*, vol. i, chap. 15.

ton production was not resorted to until there was an overproduction of tobacco, in 1660. More than once the English Kings attempted to persuade the colonists to grow grain instead of tobacco. So also, colonial legislation sought the same end, but artificial barriers could not overcome nature's predilection for tobacco. Without this fertile soil, favorably situated, the external encouragements, above enumerated, would have been fruitless.

It is commonly believed that the profits of tobacco cultivation were depended on slave labor. This was certainly not true for the planters prior to 1619, since before that date there were no slaves in Virginia. The tobacco crop, however, in that year was a large one.[1] For the first fifty years or more white indented or apprentice labor was more important than slave labor. As late as 1671 there were in Virginia three white indented apprentices to one negro slave, or six thousand of the former to two thousand of the latter, out of a total population of forty thousand.[2] When, however, the white servant labor was cut off by the increasing demand for it in those mechanical trades requiring skill, both in England and in the colonies, then cheap negro labor was a boon to the tobacco planter. So it may be said that, while the cultivation of tobacco did not in the first instance depend upon slave labor, its expansion in the eighteenth century did rest upon it. It was a fortunate coincidence for the American planter that as white labor became scarcer and dearer, negro slave labor became more plentiful and cheaper.

[1] Estimated at 20,000 lbs.

[2] According to census taken by Gov. Berkely, 1671; see Hening's *Statutes of Virginia—Statutes at Large*, vol. ii, p. 515.

We can not agree with those "abolitionists" and economists who maintained that the Southern planter was working against his best economic interests by employing slave instead of free white labor. The relative value, as a source of income to the large plantation owner, was on the side of the negro slave. The following table represents, in brief, the profits derived from the exploitation of slave labor:[1]

Annual Outlay.		Annual Return.	
1. Interest on capital invested in slaves (£50)	£2 10s.	1. Two hghds. tobacco	£16
2. Interest on farm capital required per slave	£2	2. Corn, etc.	£4
3. Living expense of slave	£3		
Total cost	£7 10s.	Total	£20

Net profit, £12 10s. per year per slave.

The net cost per slave of seven pounds ten shillings represented an investment of about one hundred pounds. The income of twenty pounds was, therefore, equivalent to twenty per cent. profit on the total capital investment, less the sum necessary to replace the fund. Just prior to the Revolutionary War the cost of maintaining a slave, seven pounds ten shillings, was low compared with the cost of a free worker per year, which was about twenty pounds (at the rate of one shilling six pence per day). As the opportunities for white labor increased with the industrial progress of the country the difference became still greater. We do not mean to maintain that the existence of tobacco cultivation was conditioned by slave labor for, as we pointed out above, cultivation had flourished before slave labor was important, and it has certainly flourished

[1] *American Husbandry*, vol. i, pp. 229, 233-234.

since the abolition of slavery. Slavery was merely a more lucrative means of exploiting the wealth of a rich and fertile soil. What cheap slave labor did do was to lower the cost of production and thereby cheapen the price of tobacco to the consumer, which in turn stimulated further consumption and cultivation. It may fairly be said that the consumer profited by this slave labor quite as much as, if not more than, the planter and landlord.

The unscientific method of cultivating tobacco, under the one-crop system, did not require more skill than the negro possessed. The planter, moreover, could not always depend on hired labor during the busy season, so that the slave labor was again an advantage over the hired help. Permanent possession of slave labor made possible constant employment throughout the year, especially where forests had to be cleared for further extension of arable land. In the manufacture of garments and the preparation of foods for plantation consumption also, the slave was serviceable. After the tobacco crop was harvested and prepared for shipment, the labor power of the slave was directed and utilized in these secondary occupations.

As the fertility of the Southern soil made the exploitation of slave labor profitable in the South, so the lack of it in the Northern colonies explains the slight development of slavery there. A number of attempts were made to grow tobacco in Massachusetts and Connecticut, as well as in New York and Pennsylvania, but they failed to produce a crop which could compete with the Southern leaf. As late as 1801 the entire New England crop was estimated at only twenty thousand pounds, or the amount which Virginia exported in 1620. Early Massachusetts records show that experiments were made to grow tobacco, but were soon abandoned as being unprofitable. In 1629, for instance, occurs the following statement: "For we find here by late experiences that it (tobacco) doth hardly produce the freight and customs duty."[1]

Along with poor soil came legal enactments, for moral reasons, against the production and consumption of tobacco in the New England colonies. Buying and selling tobacco was prohibited by law, and in some places a high sumptuary tax was levied on tobacco. All these regulations were only of secondary importance in preventing the energies of the Northern colonists from being directed to the cultivation of tobacco. As early as 1646 New Amsterdam settlers turned their attention to tobacco cultivation, but soon gave it up on account of lack of fertile soil.[2] In 1689 Pennsylvania attempted to grow tobacco, but failed for the same reason. The recent development of the industry in the Northern states begins about 1825, subsequent to the introduction of cigars and cigar leaf. But even in the cultivation of this cigar leaf, the Northern soil has to be nourished by a rich and expensive fertilizer. In the absence of the fertilizer in colonial days, Northern soil was not fitted for the tobacco crop.

We shall turn our attention next to the internal development of the industry in those colonies where it flourished most, Virginia and Maryland. In Virginia the tobacco crop and its value were the barometer that measured the material prosperity of the colony. Throughout the whole colonial period, tobacco was the chief and almost exclusive commercial crop of Virginia. In 1671

[1] *Colonial Records of Massachusetts* (compiled by N. B. Shurtleff), pp. 101, 180, 242, 388. *Ibid.*, index, "Tobacco."

[2] *Cf. Long Island Historical Society Records*, vol. i, 1679–1680; *cf.* also *American Husbandry*, vol. i, chapters 8–12.

Governor Berkely wrote in his census concerning the production of commodities, "Commodities of the growth of our country we never had any but tobacco."[1] Eighty ships came annually from England to carry tobacco to England and the continent. At this time the exportation of tobacco amounted to about 1,500,000 pounds. Just prior to the French and Indian (Seven Years) War, in 1753, export figures reached 53,862,300 pounds. A large part of the laws enacted by the Assembly, as well as many of the proclamations of the governors, are concerned with the production and sale of tobacco.

Over-production seems to have been a constant source of trouble for the Virginia planters. To check this, as well as to prevent the fall in price, numerous acts were passed by the Assembly. Prices fell from three shillings per pound in 1620, to three pence per pound in 1640. During this period, not only did the Assembly fix the price of tobacco in terms of English money, but it also fixed the price of other commodities in terms of tobacco.[2] Finding that the fixing of prices failed to remedy matters, the government tried other means of state regulation. It attempted to limit the supply by fixing the maximum number of pounds each planter could produce per cultivator employed.[3] Another method resorted to in order to increase prices, was the destruction, by government inspectors, of the poor grades of leaf. Finally, the condition of the market was so bad, and the debts of planters so high, that the Virginia Assembly declared all debts could be legally cancelled upon payment of forty per

[1] *Cf.* Hening, *Statutes of Virginia*, vol. ii, p. 514.

[2] *Ibid.*, vol. i, pp. 162, 188. *Cf.* also Burk's *History of Virginia*, vol. ii, appendix, xxvii.

[3] *Ibid.*, i, pp. 142, 152, 164, 188.

cent (forty cents on the dollar) in terms of tobacco, the price of which was already fixed by law.[1]

Having secured only temporary relief by enactments directly regulating tobacco, indirect means were resorted to. Colonial authorities, as well as Parliament, tried to induce the colonists to substitute other crops for tobacco. Flax, hemp, cotton and silk were tried but these yielded an inadequate return.[2] Even shipbuilding and trading were resorted to, but these also proved poor substitutes. The trouble with all these artificial regulations was, as the colonists themselves saw, that Maryland was able to increase her output when Virginia attempted to curtail her own. And when selling prices were fixed too high, English merchants would buy of Maryland. Besides, Spanish and Dutch traders were bringing tobacco from the West Indies to the continent. Virginia planters tried to get Maryland planters to agree to some plan whereby prices could be controlled. It was suggested that in years following heavy crops all production should cease in both colonies. Owing to mutual suspicion this plan, tried in 1666–1667, fell through. The poor farmers of Maryland, said Lord Baltimore, could not stand a year's cessation of corps, especially since their farms were mortgaged.[3] It should be added that, had the plan succeeded, Lord Baltimore would have suffered a loss in his revenues which came from tobacco export duties and a tobacco poll tax.

The statistics of production and prices for this colonial period are not complete nor always reliable. From gov-

[1] Hening, i, pp. 204, 205.

[2] Beverley's *History of Virginia*, pt. ii, c. 2, p. 233.

[3] *Cf. Archives of Maryland; Maryland Historical Society*, pp. 5–9, 15–20, 352 (years 1666–1668).

ernment figures as well as from the colonial statutes we have been able to compile the following table:

Production.		Price.	
Year.	Pounds.	Year.	Per pound.
1619	20,000	1619	3s.
1620	40,000	1620	(not known)
1621	55,000	1621	(not known)
1622	60,000	1622	(not known)
1628	500,000	1628	3d.
1639	1,500,000	1631	6d.
1641	1,300,000	1640	12d.
1688	18,157,000	1645	1½d.
1745	38,275,000	1665	1d.
1753	53,862,000	1690	2d.
1758	22,050,000	1722	¾d.
		1753	2d.
		1763	2d.

During this period of unsteady crops and over-production, resulting in violent price fluctuations, the colonists charged the home government and English merchants with being partly responsible for the depression in trade. In 1732 the Virginia Assembly embodied the protests of the planters in a petition[1] which was published and sent to the King of England. Among other things, the government is charged with imposing too high a tariff on tobacco imported into England, and the merchant is accused of charging too high commission rates. The planters also claimed that the great amount of smuggling of tobacco into England via Scotland depressed prices in England, and hence depressed the price at which it had to be sold in Virginia to English merchants. The colonists were not permitted to export their tobacco direct

[1] *The Case of the Planters of Tobacco in Virginia as Represented by Themselves, President of the Council and Burgesses*, etc. The Virginia planters laid stress upon the practice of smuggling, which was investigated by a Parliament commission.

to Europe, for the Navigation acts[1] required all shipments to be made in English vessels to England, where it was taxed before going to the continent.[2] As tobacco was among the "enumerated" articles, it had to be sold to English traders, who often agreed among themselves to depress prices. Had the entire market been open to the American planter, there would have been some relief for him. For according to Chalmer, about two-thirds of the entire crop was re-shipped from England to the continent.[3] Adam Smith puts the figure still higher. According to Smith, "about ninety-six thousand hogsheads of tobacco are annually purchased in Virginia and Maryland with a part of the surplus produce of British industry. The demand of Great Britain does not require, perhaps, more than fourteen thousand hogsheads."[4] The American planter not only suffered from the low price at which he sold his tobacco, but from the correspondingly high prices he was forced to pay for the goods he received in exchange for tobacco. On the continent, furthermore, consumption was cut down by the high price of tobacco, fixed arbitrarily by the Farmers of Revenue. This was especially true in France,[5] where tobacco was subject to monopoly throughout the eighteenth century. The cutting down of general con-

[1] Navigation acts affecting tobacco were practically in force as early as 1621. In 1624 all goods had to be carried in English ships, but it was not until the Parliamentary acts of 1651 and 1660 that this was effectively enforced.

[2] Drawbacks, however, were allowed on tobacco re-exported from England.

[3] Chalmer's *Annals*, p. 53.

[4] *Cf. Wealth of Nations*, chapter on "Different Employment of Capital."

[5] *Cf.* Arthur Young's *Present State of France*, p. 89, letter iv; also Stourm's *Le Budget*, i, p. 361.

sumption by government regulations and monopoly was, and still is, a constant source of complaint on the part of the tobacco planter.

Two special institutions, which were closely bound up with the colonial history of Virginia, the financial system and the system of land tenure, merit particular attention, inasmuch, as they rested upon, and were shaped by, the conditions of tobacco cultivation. First, as regards the financial system. Virginia did not originally and arbitrarily fix upon tobacco as a medium of exchange or as a basis of currency. Tobacco came later to hold this position, as a result of the frequent fixing of the price of tobacco. And since tobacco was the chief commercial crop, the commodities came to be reckoned in terms of tobacco. This led to the use of tobacco notes, both specific and general, which were given at the government warehouse when tobacco was stored there. The specific note called for a certain number of pounds of tobacco, of a given quality and of a given crop; whereas, the general note called for a number of pounds of tobacco of a certain grade of any crop.[1] Coin was scarce, but this entailed no great hardships, for in Virginia the plantation was usually self-sufficing and its economic life only called for few barter exchanges.[2] When we recall, however, the constant fluctuation in the price of tobacco, we can imagine what a clumsy and inefficient currency tobacco must have been. A tobacco note issued one year might lose half its value by a fall in the price of tobacco the following year.

The close relation existing between social institutions

[1] See Ripley's *Financial History of Virginia*, pp. 119-124.

[2] A vivid description of this domestic plantation economy is found in the *American Husbandry*, vol. i, pp. 226 *et seq.*

and the purely technical economic conditions, as illustrated by the currency system of colonial Virginia, is shown even more strikingly in the case of land tenure. As already hinted, the method of cultivation in the South was a capitalistic one, based on the profitableness of the plantation system, and later upon slave labor. Large estates were necessary, for tobacco was then, as now, a very exhausting crop, and hence the planter had to have an abundance of fresh land to which he could extend his cultivation. The large estate was again found profitable as a means of keeping slave labor continually employed. Hence, attached to a tobacco plantation was pasture land for cattle as well as strips of land set aside for other crops, such as grain, for plantation consumption. In a word, the cultivation of tobacco was directly responsible for the large plantation system with the accompanying opportunity for the exploitation of slave labor. A large plantation unscientifically and extensively cultivated by cheap slave labor, was more profitable than a small farm cultivated intensively by free but dear labor.[1] Along river fronts, five thousand acre plantations were quite common.[2] It was the desire to preserve intact these large estates that accounts for the institution of primogeniture in the South throughout the colonial period.

The direct and indirect effect of the tobacco industry upon other social institutions must be passed by with a brief notice. Politically, the large plantation is responsible for a representative rather than a democratic government in the southern colonies; for it was inconvenient for settlers widely scattered, as a result of the large planta-

[1] *Cf. American Husbandry*, vol. i, pp. 230–231.

[2] *Cf.* Bruce's *Economic History of Virginia*, vol. ii, pp. 253–255.

tion system, to come together as was the case in the town meeting of the New England colonies. On the fiscal side, it might be shown how the particular methods of raising revenues were resorted to because of the existence and importance of the tobacco industry.[1] The chief revenues came from an export duty and a poll tax; the export tax, besides being easily collected, was lucrative because so large a part of the chief crop of tobacco was exported. The ease with which it could be collected, and the difficulty of concealing the commodity in attempting to escape taxation, partly explains also the wide use of taxes on tobacco by the European government.[2] The poll tax was used because it was simple in its operation, and because it seemed a fairly just method of distributing the tax burden, inasmuch as a man's wealth was usually in proportion to the number of slaves he owned. Amount of rents, official salaries, ministers' fees, *et cetera*, were always payable in terms of tobacco. The extensive method of cultivation forced the colonists to seek new lands, and hence the westward expansion. In a word, the social and political history of Virginia is unintelligible apart from its economic background, the center of which was the cultivation of tobacco.

Next to Virginia in the cultivation of tobacco came Maryland. Into its detailed history we cannot enter, nor would it be profitable to do so, since in many important respects it merely repeats that of Virginia. As in Virginia, so in Maryland, it was early discovered that the fertile soil was well adapted to the cultivation of tobacco,

[1] For the relation between the tobacco industry and taxation, *cf.* Hening's *Statutes of Virginia*, vol. i, pp. 148, 226; also *cf.* Beverley's *History of Virginia*, bk. iv, c. iv.

[2] *Cf.* Adam Smith's *Wealth of Nations*, bk. i, c. xi, on Rent of Land, *passim*.

and it soon came to be the chief commercial crop. Government regulation was resorted to, as in Virginia, to maintain prices; It was frequently used as a medium of exchange.[1] It was the fear lest Maryland should become a strong competitor that influenced the Virginia tobacco planters to oppose the granting of a charter by the King to Lord Baltimore. Although it never reached the dimensions of Virginia's cultivation, Maryland's tobacco exports came to be about one-fourth of the total colonial export trade.

North Carolina also took to raising tobacco at an early date. By 1775 its export trade amounted to eighty thousand dollars, or about twenty per cent of her total exports. It was not, however, until 1850 that tobacco assumed special significance in North Carolina, the explanation of which will be given in another chapter.

At the outbreak of the American Revolution, tobacco was second on our list of exports in value, reaching in 1775 over one hundred million pounds, or about four million dollars. This product alone represented over seventy-five per cent. of the total value of goods exported from Virginia and Maryland.[2] As a result of our independence, over seventy-five per cent. of this tobacco was carried directly to the continent, no longer exclusively in English vessels or by English merchants, but by Dutch and French ships as well. England's revenues from her impost on tobacco was a handsome one. The tariff rates were very high, averaging from two hundred per cent to four hundred per cent *ad valorem* duty. As early as 1686 with a duty of four and three quarter pence per pound, (the price of tobacco being about two pence)

[1] *Cf.* Bozman's *History of Maryland*, vol. ii, pp. 78-79.

[2] *Cf. American Husbandry*, i, pp. 256-347.

she received from this source exclusively about two million dollars.[1] In 1764 the Crown of England thought it worth while to pay three hundred and fifty thousand dollars for the seignorial right over the Isle of Man to prevent smuggling into England via that place.[2] In 1700 it reached three millions five hundred thousand dollars. So far as the revenue on tobacco consumed in England is concerned, England lost nothing by our independence. Social wealth, however, she did lose by the shifting of trade profits from the pockets of English merchants to Continental merchants. The tobacco trade of Glasgow, which had been the leading tobacco center of the world, was ruined.[3]

The reader will have observed that nothing has been said thus far concerning the manufacture of tobacco. Our trade in manufactured tobacco during colonial times was a negligible quantity. We exported the raw leaf, which was afterwards manufactured abroad, not only for foreign use, but often for re-exportation to our shores. Consumption, however, in our country was not very heavy, and the products used required very simple manufacturing processes. Snuff and pipe tobacco were the principal forms of the finished product consumed. For this purpose the tobacco needed only to be ground up into a powder, or else cut up into small flakes, much as our present day pipe tobacco is prepared. There were two distinct types:[4] a "sweet scented," more expensive tobacco grown in Virginia; and the "Oronoko," a

[1] *Cf.* Parliament document *Accounts and Papers*, 1898, *Customs and Tariffs*, p. 185.

[2] *Ibid.*, p. 183. A historical sketch of the English tobacco tax is found in Stephen McDowell's *History of Taxation and Taxes in England.*

[3] McDowell's *History of Taxation and Taxes in England*, p. 256.

[4] *American Husbandry*, i, pp. 224, 225.

strong and cheaper type grown in Maryland in the Chesapeake Bay region. The more expensive type was consumed in Great Britain and at home; while the cheaper type went to Continental Europe. This is practically the distribution of our crop to-day.

Before passing to the next chapter, let us summarize the preceding sketch of the colonial period and indicate its chief lines of development. The tobacco industry received its first stimulus from external forces, chiefly the general English colonial policy, which encouraged and assisted the development of the natural resources of the colonies, and, to a lesser degree, the Bullionist financial and commercial policy which saw in the substitution of American colonial tobacco for Spanish tobacco one means of checking the exportation of silver bullion. Both of these forces, together with the economic self-interest of the King and the Virginia Company, reserved for the American planters the English tobacco market by differential tariffs; while at the same time the European markets were captured through the activity of English merchants and traders. The internal conditions upon which the progress of the industry depended were, first, an abundance of fertile land favorably situated, and, secondly, cheap slave labor. In turn, the magnitude of the industry with its plantation system and extensive methods of cultivation, reacted upon, and helped in shaping, many of the important social institutions as, for instance, land tenure, slavery, methods of taxation and financial systems. So close was this interdependence of social institutions and the tobacco industry that Chalmer is led to believe that "the story of tobacco would contain almost all the politics of the southern colonies of that age."[1] It was the tobacco industry which first

[1] Chalmer's *Annals*, i, p. 129.

helped to determine for the South its chief characteristics, an agricultural community with rich landlords on top and slave labor at the bottom. The social as well as economic structure of the South was fixed long before cotton became king. The colonial period closed with the Southern colonies supplying the world with leaf tobacco, a position which the South still holds to this day.

CHAPTER II

(1776–1860)

In the preceding chapter we have seen how tobacco came to be the chief, and almost exclusive, commercial crop of the leading Southern colonies. One-half of all the colonists in America secured their livelihood from the cultivation and sale of tobacco; and the earliest of the large fortunes in our country, namely those acquired by the landed aristocracy of the South, were founded on this exploitation of tobacco land and slave labor. One of the noteworthy incidents in this colonial period was the very rapid development that characterized the industry. In the period from 1775 to 1860 we shall see that forces came into play to check the rate of progress and to hold the production of tobacco almost stationary up to 1850; we shall learn how, in the decade from 1850 to 1860, a revival took place, how tobacco relinquished its position to cotton as the staple crop of the South and how, in the course of development, the manufacture of tobacco took root in this country. During this period, the tobacco industry did not keep pace with the progress made by the other industries, for reasons which will appear presently.

Four distinct causes operated to check the cultivation of tobacco in this country; war, the commercial policies of European countries, the revenue systems of foreign countries, and the increasing importance of cotton production. First came the disturbances occasioned by the

American Revolution, arising not only because our efforts were diverted from peaceful pursuits, but because our commerce with England, as with the rest of Europe, was crippled. It must be remembered that England was the chief buyer of our products, and war with her meant a cessation of trade. Consequently the tobacco trade suffered. Prior to the war our annual tobacco exports amounted to one hundred million pounds, whereas the average during the war was only about fifteen million pounds. It was not until 1787 that our exports approximated the pre-Revolution figures. This temporary loss of trade had a permanent effect, namely, in forcing European countries to seek their tobacco supply elsewhere. This they effected in two ways, first by encouraging growth at home, and secondly by importing tobacco from the Spanish West Indies and the Dutch East Indies. Both have continued to be competitors for the market. A similar effect was produced by the War of 1812, during which our trade was almost annihilated. The normal annual exportation of eighty thousand hogsheads fell to five thousand in 1813, and to three thousand in 1814. It was too hazardous to ship a load of tobacco, since it might easily fall a prey to an English man-of-war. Here again, the important fact was not merely the temporary loss of a few crops, but the permanent effect in giving encouragement to other than American growers of tobacco. In the twenty year period following the war (1815–1835) our exports averaged about one hundred million pounds, which really implied a retrogression in view of the augmented consumption, arising from an increased population, at home and abroad. Cuba, Colombia (S. A.), and Sumatra became active competitors, as did also some European countries, Austria, Germany and Italy.

Our foreign commerce, however, might not have suffered permanently from these war disturbances, had not the commercial policies of European countries operated in the same direction. The Napoleonic wars for a long time closed European markets to our products. The damage to our trade and commerce resulting from the Berlin and Milan Decrees, the Orders in Council and our own Embargo, is a matter of history. Our tobacco trade suffered along with the others. In 1808 our exports fell from 62,000,000 hogsheads to 9,576 hogsheads of leaf. Manufactured tobacco exports were similarly effected.[1]

Moreover, these Napoleonic wars burdened European governments, especially England and France, with heavy public debts. To wipe out these debts, import duties were greatly increased on all products partaking of the character of luxuries, including tobacco. The tobacco tax had always been considered a lucrative as well as a justifiable one. These increased duties raised the prices of tobacco to the consumer proportionately, thereby cutting down consumption, or at least checking its rate of increase. The falling off of our exports in the period subsequent to the Napoleonic wars was no doubt partly due to this factor.[2] In England, for instance, the tax was raised in 1815 on imported tobacco, from twenty-eight cents per pound to seventy-five cents per pound. This brought the duty up to nine hundred per cent *ad valorem*. England's consumption consequently fell from twenty-two million to fifteen million pounds.[3]

[1] *Cf. U. S. Census*, 1880, special report on "Manufactures of Tobacco," pp. 38, 46.

[2] Prior to 1815 our exports reached 110,000,000 hogsheads, whereas from 1815–1840 the average was about 85,000,000 hogsheads. *Cf. U. S. Census*, 1880, p. 38.

[3] See in *English Parliamentary Documents*, "Accounts and Papers,"

The English duties were so high that a special committee was appointed by Parliament to investigate the disturbed conditions of trade resulting from the increased tax.[1] This committee reported that the prices of tobacco were so high that smuggling and adulteration of tobacco were made very profitable. The American Chamber of Commerce of Liverpool presented a petition to the committee requesting a reduction of duties on tobacco, on the ground that consumption, and hence trade, would increase for England and the United States.[2] This Parliamentary investigation committee declared its belief that "the annals of taxation do not exhibit an instance of such a heavy impost in any country as the present duty on tobacco." (Nine hundred per cent *ad valorem.*) The like was true, though not to the same extent, in France, Austria, Spain and Italy, where the "Régie" was in vogue, and the government fixed prices arbitrarily. In our own country the best snuff or manufactured tobacco could be bought at retail in 1840, for twenty-five cents per pound; whereas, the price in England was seventy-five cents per pound for snuff and forty-five for manufactured tobacco; and in France the retail price was thirty-five cents per pound for the ordinary tobacco of both kinds used.

These high duties not only checked per capita consumption, but stimulated further production in European countries, since the farmer was protected from American

"Customs and Tariffs" (1898), p. 38. These figures, however, are in part vitiated by the great amount of smuggling which resulted directly from the increased duty.

[1] "Report from a Select Committee on the Tobacco Trade," report 565, year 1844, *Parliamentary Documents*.

[2] *Ibid.*, pp. 95-97.

competition. At the close of the eighteenth century, tobacco cultivation was almost unknown in European countries. By 1841, however, the total production of Europe had reached 136,680,000 pounds, which was about sixty per cent of our own crop, 219,000,000 lbs., in 1840.[1] The competition in the leaf market from non-European markets came from Cuba, Colombia, Porto Rico and the East Indies.[2] The general relation between taxation and consumption will be treated in detail in another connection.

More important than any or all of the above checks and discouragements to our tobacco trade, was the rising importance of cotton culture in our Southern states. The low price of cotton goods, effected by a cheapening in the cost of producing the raw material as well as the finished products, through technical improvements, led to an increased demand for cotton and hence for cotton land. Not only was there a demand for land but for slave labor as well, for the profits of cotton culture were more alluring than those of tobacco cultivation. Cotton culture affected in this double way the cost of producing tobacco: for an increase in land values meant a rise in rents, and an increase in the value of slave labor meant a higher cost in wages necessary for tobacco pro-

[1] *European Production of Leaf in 1844:*

Germany	40,000,000 lbs.
Austria	35,000,000 lbs.
France	26,000,000 lbs.
Russia	21,000,000 lbs.

[2] *Imports into England in 1841:*

From United States	34,628,000
From Colombia	785,000
From East Indies	223,347
From Cuba	259,702
From Porto Rico	146,000

duction. Unless the price of tobacco rose, cultivation would cease on some lands. Not only were uncultivated fields, bought originally for tobacco production, given over to cotton culture, but tobacco plantations were converted into cotton fields. In 1790 cotton exports were valued at five hundred thousand dollars, in 1800 at eleven million dollars. From that year cotton cultivation has gone on rapidly and has displaced tobacco as the chief crop of the South.

But while the industry itself suffered from this growing importance of the cotton crop, the owners of tobacco plantations and slave owners profited directly by the change. They suddenly found that the value of their land and slaves had doubled.[1] It should be remembered that the system of cultivation on plantations and by slave labor, originated and developed under tobacco cultivation, was taken over by cotton growers. Since the profitableness of the system had been demonstrated in the one case, why should it not prove so in the other?

Other forces, however, were at work counteracting the effect of these discouraging influences. Not only had population increased, and with it the demand for tobacco, but the general command over purchasing power in all commodities had risen during this period of prosperity. This was certainly true of our American society, if not of Europe. Moreover, consumption was directly stimulated

[1] According to W. B. Phillips the value of slaves was as follows:

1773-1790	$300 per capita.
1800	$450 per capita.
1809	$600 per capita.
1837	$1,300 per capita.
1860	$1,800 per capita.

Cf. "The Economic Cost of Slave-Holding," in *Political Science Quarterly*, vol. xx, 1905.

by improvement in the quality as well as in the outward appearance of tobacco. New methods of "curing"[1] tobacco gave rise to a sweeter as well as a brighter and hence more attractive leaf. Prior to 1812 curing was done in the open air; subsequent to that date a wood fire was employed. Later, in 1837, charcoal was used. These technical processes made possible the introduction of an entirely new leaf, the "Yellow Bright," which almost revolutionized the leaf market. In 1852 a lemon leaf was grown for the first time in North Carolina (Caswel County), which at once became popular in foreign as well as in home markets. It not only displaced some of the darker types, but increased the consumption of tobacco in all forms and all types. Production increased in a single decade (1850–1860) about one hundred and fifteen per cent,[2] or from 200,000,000 pounds in 1849 to 434,000,000 pounds in 1859.

The immediate effect of the introduction and popularity of this new leaf, used for plug fillers and wrappers, was to send land values in North Carolina sky high. The loose porous soil of Person, Granville and Rockingham counties, though arid and unfertile for other crops, was well adapted to tobacco.[3] Mr. Killebrew, a tobacco expert, says that land values rose from fifty cents to fifty dollars per acre. The relative crop values in that decade were estimated per acre, eight dollars for corn, fifteen dollars for cotton, and fifty dollars for tobacco.

From North Carolina the cultivation of this new leaf was extended to Kentucky, Ohio and Tennessee. The

[1] Curing is the process whereby the moist green leaf is forced through a process of fermentation in order to sweeten it and give it a rich brown or yellow color.

[2] *Cf. United States Census*, 1840, 1850 and 1880.

[3] It contained plenty of sodium but little plant nutrition.

following table shows the progress made from 1850 to 1860:[1]

PRODUCTION OF LEAF.

	1849. Pounds.	1859. Pounds.	Increase per cent.
North Carolina	11,964,786	32,853,250	200
Ohio	10,454,449	25,092,581	150
Tennessee	20,148,932	43,488,097	115
Virginia	56,803,227	123,968,312	100
Kentucky	55,501,196	108,126,840	97
Maryland	21,407,497	38,410,965	80

That this remarkable progress was partly due to a general increase in tobacco consumption may be inferred from the fact that a similar development took place in the growing of cigar leaf in the Northern states, as indicated in the following table:

PRODUCTION OF NORTHERN CIGAR LEAF.

	1849. Pounds.	1859. Pounds.	Increase per cent.
Connecticut	1,267,624	6,000,000	400
Pennsylvania	912,651	3,181,000	245
Massachusetts	138,246	3,233,198	3000
New York	83,189	5,764,582	7000

During the entire period up to 1860 no great change took place in the method of cultivation. It was still largely the unscientific and extensive system, that is, one crop and no rotation, which was fast impoverishing the soil. The ordinary natural fertilizer was too expensive, and commercial fertilizer did not come into the market until 1840. In that year guano was imported from South America. By 1860 the United States was using over one thousand tons of guano, much of which went into tobacco fields. It was the use of artificial commercial fertilizer

[1] Based on Tenth and Twelfth Census.

that made possible the production of a cigar leaf in Northern states. The South was still the tobacco producing section, not only of our country but of the world. In 1860 five states produced seventy-five per cent of our entire crop. The following table gives by percentages the yield by states for three decades:[1]

PERCENTAGE OF TOBACCO CROP OF THE UNITED STATES GROWN BY PRINCIPAL STATES, 1839-1859.

	CENSUS YEAR.		
	1839. Per cent.	1849. Per cent.	1859. Per cent.
Virginia	34.4	28.4	28.6
Kentucky	24.4	27.8	24.9
Tennessee	13.5	10.1	10.0
Maryland	11.3	10.7	8.9
North Carolina	7.7	6.0	7.6
Ohio	2.7	5.3	5.8
Connecticut and Massachusetts	.2	.7	2.2
New York		.1	1.3

In 1860 our total crop approximated four hundred million pounds, more than one-half of which was exported to Europe. We still maintained our position, acquired during the colonial period, as the largest tobacco supplying market of the world. In order to avoid paying the duty on the useless stems, which forms about ten per cent of the total weight of tobacco, leaf shipped to England was stripped of the mid-rib.

Not only were we in control of the leaf market, but we were beginning to show signs of activity in the manufacture of tobacco. During colonial times we imported finished products, snuff and pipe tobacco from England. But as early as 1825 we were sending manufactured products to England. England aided us in securing a foot-

[1] *Cf. Tobacco* (trade journal), May, 1906, anniversary edition, containing a statistical survey.

hold in continental markets by imposing a high duty on leaf which, because of a loss in weight when manufactured, put English manufactures at a disadvantage[1] Our exports of manufactured products prior to 1790 were nil; since that year the movement has been a progressively favorable one. The following table shows its progress from 1790 to 1860:

EXPORTS OF MANUFACTURES.

Year	Quantity	Year	Quantity
1790	81,000 lbs.	1830	3,199,000 lbs.
1800	457,000 lbs.	1840	6,787,943 lbs.
1810	495,000 lbs.	1850	7,010,000 lbs.
1820	593,000 lbs.	1860	17,697,000 lbs.

This is exclusive of snuff. The principal items of export were smoking (pipe) tobacco and chewing tobacco. These were machine-made products, and because the labor-cost was not important, we were able to compete abroad. In the sale of cigars, wherein hand labor is important, however, it was otherwise. German manufacturers, with cheaper labor, easily undersold us. Prior to the enactment of the high tariff of 1862, which practically shut out foreign goods, we imported from Germany annually upward to five million dollars worth of cigars. The value of imported cigars was greater than the total value of our exported manufactured tobacco products. In the five year period (1855–1860) our annual imports were valued at four million dollars, while our exports were only about two million dollars. Manufactured tobacco was made chiefly in Richmond, St. Louis, Lynchburg, Petersburg, Louisville and New Orleans. The principal cigar centers were New York City and Philadelphia. Cigars were made exclusively by hand, and

[1] It took, for instance, 114 lbs. of raw leaf to make 100 lbs. of finished product. The duty was paid on 114 lbs., but the drawback on 100 lbs. With a 900 per cent *ad valorem* duty, this loss was very heavy.

under the domestic system of production. Up to the Civil War the principal form of tobacco consumption was pipe tobacco. This was the cheapest form of indulgence, and hence popular among the poorer classes. Snuff and cigars were more expensive, the latter being used almost exclusively by the richer classes. Even to-day the cigar is the most expensive form of tobacco consumption. Owing to the uncertain character of statistics, the rate and volume of consumption cannot be accurately estimated for this period. In our chapter on "Consumption," however, we shall refer to this point.

In the eighty-five years thus briefly sketched, we have seen how the rate of progress in the development of the industry was temporarily checked by the commercial disturbances of the Revolutionary War and the War of 1812; how this temporary check reacted permanently by encouraging cultivation in Europe, Central and South America, and the East Indies; how the blockading of European ports during the Napoleonic wars led to the same result; how heavy import duties, to wipe out the debts occasioned by those wars, affected permanently the consumption, and thereby the production of tobacco, and lastly, how the profitableness of cotton production relegated tobacco to the background. In the final decade of the period, the industry revived through the increased consumption stimulated by a more desirable and attractive tobacco, the "Yellow Bright" of North Carolina. Not only were we supplying raw leaf to the world but, in addition to supplying ourselves with all forms of manufactured tobacco, we entered foreign markets in the sale of finished products. It is, however, in the period since the Civil War that the industry has shown most rapid development in all its forms, in agriculture as well as manufactures.

PART II—MODERN PERIOD: 1860-1905

CHAPTER I

Consumption

It is not with the moral aspect of the problem that we are here concerned. Yet, from a social standpoint, the economist can not ignore the effect of consumption upon the working efficiency of the individual. The special problems, for which statistical data are available and which will receive consideration are: first, the extent and tendency of consumption; second, the consumption of tobacco compared with other commodities; third, the social importance of tobacco from the point of view of national expenditure, as well as of that of the family budget; fourth, the more important conditions upon which the rate and extent of consumption depend, such as general purchasing power, prices, taxation, and legislation.

With the possible exception of Belgium, United States is the heaviest consumer of tobacco among all the western nations. Our consumption has kept pace with the growing material prosperity of the country. The use of tobacco has been further stimulated not only by a relative decrease in price but also by the increasing superior quality of the finished products offered for sale. The mere superficial attractiveness of the cigar has, from a psychological standpoint, stimulated its consumption in recent years. Whatever the reasons may be, statistics for the last fifty years show a remarkable growth in per capita consumption in the United States, as seen in the following table:[1]

ANNUAL PER CAPITA CONSUMPTION IN THE UNITED STATES.

Years.	Pounds.	Years.	Pounds.
1863-1865	1.6	1886-1890	4.6
1866-1870	1.8	1891-1895	5.1
1871-1875	3.2	1896-1900	5.3
1876-1880	3.2	1900-1905	5.5
1881-1885	4.3		

This represents an increase of two hundred and forty per cent since the Civil War.[2] In the same period consumption in European countries shows nothing like this rate of increase, as appears in the following table:[3]

PERCENTAGE INCREASE PER CAPITA CONSUMPTION, 1860-1905.

United States	240 per cent.	France	24 per cent.
England	56 per cent.	Germany	23 per cent.

The following table presents the comparative per capita consumption for these countries since 1860, from which it appears that since 1880, our consumption has far exceeded that of other countries: [4]

[1] Based on the annual reports of the Commissioner of Internal Revenue and the United States Statistical Abstract.

[2] In view of the shifting proportion of males and females to the entire population, the figures based on per capita consumption are not a strictly accurate basis, but the change has not been great enough seriously to affect the above average.

[3] Statistics for foreign countries have in each case been compiled from government documents of the respective countries.

[4] *Ibid.*

ANNUAL PER CAPITA CONSUMPTION.

	1860 to 1865. lbs.	1866 to 1870. lbs.	1871 to 1875. lbs.	1876 to 1880. lbs.	1881 to 1885. lbs.	1886 to 1890. lbs.	1891 to 1895. lbs.	1896 to 1900. lbs.	1901 to 1905. lbs.
United States	1.6	1.8	3.2	3.2	4.3	4.6	5.1	5.3	5.5
Germany	2.8	2.8	3.9	3.7	3.0	3.3	3.3	3.5	3.5
France	1.7	1.8	1.7	1.9	2.0	2.0	2.1	2.1	2.1
England	1.2	1.3	1.3	1.4	1.3	1.4	1.6	1.8	1.9

Consumption in Austria-Hungary is about three pounds per capita, in Russia one and two-tenths pounds, and in Italy only one pound per capita. For Belgium the rate is very high, about five and one-half pounds. The high consumption figure for our own country must be discounted not only because of our higher male population, but also because the particular form of consumption, chewing and smoking tobacco, so heavy in this country, is adulterated to the extent of about twenty per cent. of its weight with foreign ingredients, like sugar, flavors and licorice. The five and one-half pounds per capita for the total population, represents sixteen pounds per male above sixteen years of age. This, in turn, is equivalent to a weekly consumption of four cigars, two cigarettes and four ounces of smoking and chewing tobacco, with an average cost of thirty cents per week per capita.

It may be interesting to note what particular forms this consumption assumes. Until 1870 cigars and cigarettes were only in slight demand compared with smoking and chewing tobacco. More recently, however, the tendency has been strongly in favor of cigars and cigarettes, and more especially of the former. From 1880 to 1897 cigarettes were very popular, but since then they have fallen in importance. The following tables show the development in the last twenty-five years:

ANNUAL PER CAPITA CONSUMPTION OF VARIOUS FORMS OF TOBACCO.

	Plug, smoking, chewing tobacco.		Cigars.		Cigarettes.	
	Lbs.	Per cent. increase.	Lbs.	Per cent. increase.	Lbs	Per cent. increase.
1880–1885 ..	1.25		.3		.06	
1901–1905 ..	3.80	200	1.4	300	.18	200

In order to appreciate what this rate of consumption implies, we present in the following table the actual quantity of leaf consumed in plug, chewing and smoking tobacco, as well as the total number of cigars and cigarettes consumed in two five-year periods since 1890:

TOTAL ANNUAL QUANTITY CONSUMED.

	Plug, smoking, chewing tobacco.	Cigars.	Cigarettes.
1890–1895	266,400,000	4,300,000,000	3,555,000,000
1900–1905	312,500,000	6,360,000,000	3,000,000,000

Inasmuch as the cigar is the most expensive form of tobacco consumed, the increased consumption as shown in the rate and the absolute quantity of cigars consumed is proof of the expansion and extension of the general purchasing power of the community. Our social wealth, or general purchasing power, seems to have been *extensively* distributed, otherwise the point of satiety, for the individual, would have prevented the above increase, at least in the weight of the leaf consumed. Beyond a certain point, increased purchasing power does not mean, for the individual, more consumption, but consumption of a finer and higher quality.

It is surprising to learn what a large part of our social income is spent annually for tobacco. According to the *Census of Manufactures* (Bulletin 57, 1905, U. S.), the wholesale value of the product manufactured is about $330,000,000, which when retailed would easily amount to $425,000,000. Add to this the value of imported goods ($12,000,000) and the product of small domestic factories not included in the census, and we have in round numbers nearly $500,000,000. On the basis of quantity consumed, and the retail price roughly estimated, this expenditure is distributed as follows:

ANNUAL EXPENDITURE.

	Quantity.	Retail price Per unit.	Total retail price. Expenditure.
Cigars (number)	7,000,000,000	$50 per M.	$350,000,000
Mfg. tobacco (lbs.)	335,000,000	40 cts. per lb.	135,000,000
Cigarettes (number)	3,000,000,000	$5 per M.	15,000,000
		Total expenditure	$500,000,000

If these figures based on the census reports are correct, there is more money spent annually for tobacco than for any one of the following commodities: men's clothing, boots and shoes, furniture, gas and petroleum, hosiery and knit goods.

The significance of this tobacco expenditure is more easily grasped when we consider its part in the family budget. Of the 25,440 family budgets analyzed, 2,567 were selected for the purpose of showing expenditure for liquor, tobacco, et cetera, of which the following is a brief summary.[1]

	Percentage reporting consumption.	Average expenditure per family.	Percentage of total expenditure.
Liquors	50.72	$24.53	3.1 per cent.
Tobacco........................	79.20	13.80	1.8 per cent.
Books—Newspapers	94.74	8.82	1.1 per cent.

[1] *Cf. Eighteenth Annual Report, Bureau of Labor* (U. S.), 1903.

If these figures are a criterion, then out of each dollar expended, five cents are for liquor and tobacco; two cents going for tobacco alone.

On the basis of this same report, other interesting deductions can be drawn. For instance, it appears that industrial families spend for tobacco much more than agricultural families, $11.63 in western states and $18.19 in north central states. The farming classes, however, may consume cheaper goods and thus compensate in quantity for lack in quality. Or it may indicate that the purchasing power in industrial families is greater than in agricultural families. The character of city life in general stimulates tobacco consumption. It has been found that families having the heaviest consumption of liquor report the greatest amount of tobacco consumption.[1]

All statistics seem to point to one conclusion, that tobacco has become a fixed charge in the budget of the tobacco consumer. Although not a necessary of life in the same sense that bread and clothes are, tobacco is no longer regarded as a luxury. In a period of thirty years the demand has not only not suffered a decline, but its rate per capita has augmented. This can not be said even of those commodities which are regarded as of greater necessity, such as wheat, cotton and coffee. Tobacco consumption suffers very slightly in periods of depression, while its rate of increase is gradual in periods of prosperity.

The effect of a variation in price on the rate of consumption is difficult to trace. This is especially true in the tobacco industry where retail prices remain constant owing to the convenience of the customary price, five cents and multiples of five. When raw material (the leaf)

[1] *Cf. Eighteenth Annual Report, Bureau of Labor* (U. S.), 1903, p. 5.

advances in price, or labor costs rise, the increase is not always reflected in the retail price, but in the quantity or quality of the goods offered for sale at the old price. Furthermore, when the price variation is a slight one, it is often borne by the intermediate jobbers, whose profits admit of such fluctuation. For instance, in the last three years the price of cigar leaf has risen on an average about fifty per cent, increasing the net cost of production at least ten per cent. Yet retail prices and often wholesale prices, have not changed in the least. It was the manufacturer and jobber who shared the loss between them; though frequently an inferior product was offered to the consumer, the substitution was too slight to affect the rate of consumption.

When, however, the influence affecting price is a more permanent one, as a high tariff or internal revenue tax, then the reaction upon consumption is more noticeable. For instance, in the period from 1865 to 1868 when our internal revenue tax was increased from eleven cents to thirty cents per pound, consumption fell from one and three-tenths pounds to one pound per capita.[1] The increase in the tax, during the Spanish-American War, on "manufactured tobacco" from six to twelve cents per pound, was accompanied by a decrease in consumption from three and nine-tenths to three and three-tenths per capita. We have purposely selected cases where the increase in the tax was sufficiently high to affect prices, avoiding the question as to the incidence of the tax, a problem which will be discussed in another chapter. Here we are concerned only with the relation between consumption and prices. Assuming that a high tax does

[1] See B. W. Arnold's *Tobacco Industry in Virginia*. Mr. Arnold attributes the "slump" in the Southern tobacco industry to the rise in the tax.

reflect itself in the net price, the difference in consumption among various countries having different tax rates is significant. The following table shows this relation:

1900–1905.

	Tax per pound.	Consumption. Per capita.
Belgium	38 cents	5.75
United States	15 cents	5.30
Germany	8 cents	3.52
Austria	34 cents	3.02
Hungary	29 cents	2.45
France	76 cents	2.12
United Kingdom	76 cents	1.93
Russia	16 cents	1.20
Italy	91 cents	1.02

That is to say, where the tax is low as in the United States, Belgium and Germany consumption is heaviest; whereas, in countries where the tax is high, consumption is lowest, as in Italy, England, France. Taxation, therefore, through its influence on price, is an effective means of regulating consumption.

An important factor determining the consumption of tobacco, but one which can not be studied statistically, is the change in fashion. For instance, among the German students use of tobacco has partially displaced the use of liquors, not because of any alteration in the price or even in the quality of tobacco, but simply because of a whimsical change in the social attitude towards the use of tobacco. Similarly, a loosening of the prevailing moral code may often stimulate the consumption of tobacco. It is, however, beyond the scope of this chapter to examine all the forces that influence consumption. The problem of substitution, which is always active in affecting the demand for tobacco, is an interesting one. It has been observed that the cheapness and attractiveness of other pleasures, somewhat akin to tobacco consumption, tends to curtail the latter where the purchasing ability of the consumer does not permit him to enjoy both; where, however, the general purchasing power admits both, the consumption of the one leads to, or encourages, the other. Again, national customs and traditions have also affected the use of tobacco, and its introduction, once effected, supplants other commodities. The Tobacco Trust, for instance, is educating the Chinese people to the use of our western tobacco, with the possibility of supplanting their own.

In our own country, legislative enactments have been resorted to in order to check the consumption of tobacco. There is scarcely a state or territory that has not, in one form or another, some prohibitory provision concerning the sale or consumption of tobacco either to minors or to adults. Anti-cigarette laws have been on the statute books of Indiana, Iowa, Nebraska, Tennessee, Wisconsin and other states, but to no avail. Just why this agitation should be aimed solely at cigarettes is not clear, for medical experts maintain that the most injurious form is pipe tobacco, which leaves in the bowl of the pipe both nicotine and paradine. Scientific investigations have not yet proven that cigarettes, when taken moderately, are physiologically injurious.[1]

For good or for bad, United States leads the world in the consumption of tobacco, and the rate of increase in our country has been most rapid in the last fifty years. Our annual expenditure approximates five hundred million dollars, which involves the continual employment of

[1] *Cf. Cigarettes in Fact and Fancy*, published by H. M. Caldwell Co., Boston. *Cf. Lancet* (Medical Journal), 1905. *Cf.* Killibrew and Myrick, *Tobacco Leaf*, chap. ii.

about five hundred thousand men, women and children. In the budget of the family as of the individual, tobacco has come to occupy an increasingly important place, until indeed, it may be classed among the poor man's necessaries. The chief cause for the magnitude and rate of consumption is the growing material wealth of the country, which, judged from the weight of tobacco consumed, has been *extensive*. Temporary price fluctuations do not register themselves in the rate of consumption; but permanent influences in prices, as a high tax, do affect consumption. For we observed that countries having the highest rate of taxation had also the lowest rate of consumption, those having the lowest rate of taxation had the highest rate of consumption. It is the cultivation of tobacco and its problems, that we shall discuss in the next chapter.

CHAPTER II

Cultivation of Tobacco—Agrarian Problems

The peculiar character of the tobacco crop, the various methods of cultivating it and the different "curing" processes by which it may be treated, are in no small degree responsible for the problems that beset the planter. While it is a crop that requires unusual skill and a relatively large capital investment, its returns are hazardous and uncertain. Its commercial value depends largely upon the success or failure of some seemingly simple process, such as preparing the seed-bed, setting, worming, topping, or suckering the plant. Finally, after the crop is harvested it must be subjected to a process of leaf-fermentation, called "curing," which often determines its grade and selling value. In what follows we shall first describe briefly those steps in cultivation which must be understood in order to appreciate the broader economic problems which we shall next consider.

Every tobacco-growing section, and each type of leaf, has its distinctive method of cultivation; but we can do no more than treat of some typical processes common to all. First comes a very careful preparation of a seed-bed in which plants are raised, like hothouse vegetables, for "transplantation" later to the field. Though the seed-bed is small (about two square yards for each acre of cultivation) its preparation is both important and costly. The ground in the seed-bed must be weeded and often burned in order to destroy bacteria; and finally it must be heavily fertilized. It is covered over, usually with glass, for protection against obnoxious insects and sudden climatic changes. The expense in the construction and operation of a seed-bed is estimated at about three per cent of the total cost of production per acre. In Cuba this raising of young plants has become a specialized form of agriculture, which has resulted in the production of a finer plant at less expense. This seed-bed preparation requires from six to eight weeks.

In the meantime the ground is broken, ploughed and harrowed several times. The field is then marked off in parallel ridges about three feet apart, and in each row are heaped up, at uniform intervals (15 inches apart) small mounds of earth to receive the plants without danger of the latter being washed away by heavy rain During the entire period from the setting of the plants until harvesting time, constant weeding is required. The production of a fine crop necessitates no less than six different "cultivations" (in the technical sense). As soon as the stalk has reared its head high enough it must be "topped," a pinching off of the top buds in order to concentrate the strength of the stalk into fewer leaves. The lower or ground leaves are removed for the same purpose, as are also the subsidiary shoots growing out from the axis of the plant. The former is called "priming," the latter "suckering." All these processes, together with "worming," require plenty of labor employed constantly, for about three months, up to harvesting time. As every stalk must be cut down singly by a hand knife, even harvesting is costly. The net labor-expense from the setting of the plants through harvesting, forms about fifty per cent of the total cost of production.

When harvested, the leaf is green and odorless and is

not considered *tobacco* until "cured" by a sweating process which gives it its agreeable color and flavor. Though the methods of curing vary, the principle is the same; natural or artificial heat is used to increase the activity of the bacilli, which, by some chemical process, expel from the leaf the disagreeable sap, leaving uninjured the juices that give flavor to the leaf. There are three distinct methods of curing. In several counties of Virginia north of the James River and northeast of Richmond, tobacco is "sun-cured." On the other hand "white Burley" of Kentucky, as well as the cigar leaf of the North, is cured by the "air-drying" process. For this purpose barns or tobacco houses are constructed wherein ventilation can be carefully regulated; the purpose being to keep the air as dry as possible during the curing season.

The tobacco is suspended on poles in a position to take advantage of the incoming currents of air. Two to four months are required to cure the leaf by this "air" process. Artificial heat is resorted to only when the air seems too damp. A third method is that in which the curing depends solely on artificial heat, as in the "heavy shipping" districts of western Tennessee and Kentucky. This artificial heat may be applied in two ways: either by open fires or by flues. In the former case a wood fire is built directly under the tobacco stalks suspended on scaffolds. Three or four days' constant heating is sufficient to "cure" the leaf and prepare it for foreign shipments. By this "open-fire" process the pores of the leaf are surcharged with a carbonaceous substance which gives it a strong flavor and deprives it of its natural absorptive capacity. The Europeans prefer this leaf. The "yellow" tobacco of North Carolina, used for cigarettes and smoking tobacco, is cured either by this "open-fire" method, charcoal being the usual fuel, or by "flues." In the latter case pipes are constructed around the inside walls of the barn and supplied with heat from a furnace located near the curing "house." Since each stage in the curing process requires varying degrees of heat, the merit of this flue system consists in the fact that the temperature can be scientifically regulated. As each mode of curing demands different amounts and kinds of labor, as well as dissimilar capital investment for mechanical aid, the cost or expense of curing cannot be averaged. The wear and tear and the interest charges on the "barn" amount to ten dollars per acre. In the "sun-cured" process the cost is slight since little labor is needed and less capital than in the "air-cure" method which necessitates not only an original capital investment but also a greater quantity of labor. For whereas the former can be completed in three or four days, the latter requires from two to four months. After the tobacco is cured it is sorted and graded, and often packed, by the grower, in preparation for the market.

Despite the obstacles that attend the raising of tobacco its cultivation in 1900 was reported in no less than forty-five states and territories. In eighteen states over 1,000,000 lbs. were harvested, and in several states—Kentucky, North Carolina, Tennessee, Virginia, Connecticut—it was one of the principal commercial crops. There were, in 1900, no less than 300,000 farms growing some tobacco for the market, and for 100,000 of these tobacco represented forty per cent of the entire income. In the census enumeration these latter are grouped as "tobacco farms." The leaf cultivated in this wide area can be broadly classed under either cigar leaf or "manufacturing tobacco" leaf.[1] The former is almost ex-

[1] The term is ambiguous, but we use it because of its traditional con-

clusively a product of the Northern States and is used for fillers, binders, or wrappers solely in the manufacture of cigars: the latter is a Southern product and used in the the manufacture of plug, chewing and smoking tobacco, snuff and cigarettes. While the cigar leaf can be utilized for the latter purposes, the manufacturing leaf can be used only in the production of the cheapest grade of cigars and stogies. In the following table we present a classification of the leaf market as it appears to the manufacturer:

CLASSIFICATION OF LEAF TOBACCO.

Class.	*Where cultivated.*
CIGAR LEAF.	
Fillers	Connecticut, Ohio, New York, Pennsylvania (also to slight extent in Florida, Georgia, Texas).
Binders	Wisconsin, Pennsylvania, Connecticut.
Wrappers	Connecticut, Florida.
PLUG.	
Fillers	Kentucky, Ohio, Tennessee, Missouri, Illinois. (Known as Burley Leaf.)
Wrappers	Virginia, North Carolina, Kentucky.
Chewing tobacco	Burley Leaf.
Pipe-smoking tobacco	North Carolina, South Carolina, Eastern Virginia, Eastern Tennessee.
Cigarette leaf	Same as smoking tobacco above (North Carolina, Eastern Virginia, South Carolina, Eastern Tennessee).
Snuff	Blend or mixture of various types.

All finished tobacco products are made more or less of blends or combinations of several kinds of leaf. Each manufacturer learns by experience what "blend" best suits his particular market. This is especially true of snuff; every producer has some secret manufacturing

notation. Manufacturing leaf is that used in machine-made products such as plug, chewing and smoking tobacco.

process to which he attributes the superior quality of his particular brand. The peculiar characteristic of nearly all of the southern leaf is its absorptive capacity which enables the manufacturer to adulterate the raw material (leaf) to no less than twenty per cent of its original weight. Adulteration is here not used in a bad sense, since the admixture of foreign ingredients, licorice, sugar, and flavors of various kinds, is considered an essential part of the manufacturing process. The cigar leaf depends almost entirely upon its natural taste and aroma. Some cigar manufacturers, however, do flavor their leaf.

The old extensive method of cultivation, yielding quick returns at the expense of the soil, is gradually being displaced by intensive cultivation. This tendency began with the abolition of slave labor. With a permanent supply of labor no longer available the landowner frequently found himself in possession of a vast estate often unused but always heavily taxed. This perplexity has made necessary the leasing or selling of small portions of the land. Since it is profitable to get as heavy a yield as possible from every acre put to cultivation, small holdings, whether tilled by tenants or by owners directly, tend naturally to an intensive working of the land. Under the plantation system with large estates operated by cheap slave labor, the owner was content with a large crop from soil worked superficially. This breaking-up of the large estates into small holdings has been accentuated by the existence of what might be termed "absentee landlordism." The industrial development of the South since the Civil War has stimulated a steady migration from the farm to the city on the part not only of laborers, but also of wealthy landowners in search of superior economic as well as social and educational opportunities which the city offers. The result is that the landlords continue to exercise, from a distance only, a loose supervision over their estates, which in due time leads to a loss of interest in farming. Gradually the old landed aristocracy is losing its position by surrendering at first only direct control, but finally possession of its estates to small owners. Prior to 1860, in Virginia, where tobacco was the chief crop, the average tobacco farm ranged from 100 to 500 acres; to-day in the same districts the average is from 20 to 50 acres.[1] In the leading tobacco states since the war, Kentucky, North Carolina, Virginia and Tennessee, the number of twenty-acre tobacco farms has greatly increased since 1860.

On small as well as on large fields, intensive farming has of course been hastened, as well as made possible, by improvements in methods of cultivation. The utilization of commercial fertilizers and a scientific rotation of crops have enabled the planter to increase enormously the yield per acre.

The following table shows clearly the tendency towards intensive cultivation since 1880 in the leading tobacco states:

PERCENTAGE INCREASE OF ACREAGE AND YIELD PER ACRE, FROM 1880 TO 1900.

	Percentage acreage increase.	Percentage crop increase.
Kentucky	70 per cent.	84 per cent.
North Carolina	250 per cent.	375 per cent.
Virginia[1].	31 per cent.	53 per cent.

[1] Compare the acreage per farm in the following tobacco counties of Virginia in 1860 and 1900: Charlotte, Albemarle, Prince Edward, Mecklenberg, Louisa, Lunenberg, Pittsylvania, Augusta. *Cf. U. S. Census, 1860*, pp. 218–19; *U. S. Census, 1900, Part II, Agriculture*, pp. 53, 125.

The following table represents the increase in the actual yield in several Southern States since 1880:

YIELD PER ACRE.

	1880.	1905.
Kentucky	757 lbs.	830 lbs.
North Carolina	472 lbs.	608 lbs.
Virginia	568 lbs.	675 lbs.
Tennessee	707 lbs.	768 lbs.

These figures indicate an increase in the yield of 90 pounds per acre (from 630 pounds to 720 pounds). Recent experiments conducted by the United States Bureau of Agriculture prove conclusively the profitableness of a judicious use of artificial fertilizers, especially in Virginia, where the soil has become exhausted from continued use. The results of one of these scientific investigations for the purpose of showing the utility of fertilizers are summarized in the following table:[1]

	Cost of fertilizer.	Cost of production.	Selling price.	Profit.
Field A	$5.00	$40.00	$45.50	12½ per cent.
Field B	16.00	60.00	81.09	34 per cent.
Field C	32.00	80.00	111.29	39 per cent.

With an ever cheapening cost of fertilization, the impoverished Virginia soil may some day be restored to its ancient standard of productivity. In the Northern States this intensive cultivation has been carried on successfully for a number of years. The land of the Connecticut and Housatonic Valleys is yielding to-day, with the aid of fertilizers, twice as much per acre as the Southern land with which in Colonial days it could not compete. For instance in 1906 the yield per acre for Massachusetts and

[1] *Cf. Year-Book of the U. S. Dept. of Agriculture*, 1905, pp. 222–224.

Connecticut was 1,750 pounds, as against 870 and 580 pounds respectively for Kentucky and Tennessee. Into the tobacco districts of the Connecticut and Housatonic Valleys are shipped annually a thousand car-loads of barn manure from Boston and New York. Ordinary barn manure is very valuable as a tobacco fertilizer because it contains some amount of nearly all the principal ingredients, nitrogen, phosphoric acid, potash, lime and magnesia. The principal ingredient, nitrogen, is obtained from cotton seed meal, castor pomace, linseed meal, sulphate of ammonia and nitrate of soda. The complaint is made that our commercial fertilizers do not contain the elements that are claimed for them; they are deficient in nitrogen and potash and contain too much acid phosphates. Commercial fertilizers are used more extensively in the North than in the South; in the former about two tons per acre. The following figures show the relative importance of fertilizers for Northern and Southern tobacco farms:[1]

	Fertilizers, cost per farm.
Massachusetts	$227.00
Connecticut	218.00
South Carolina	66.00
North Carolina	42.00
Virginia	34.00
Maryland	36.00
Tennessee	17.00
Kentucky	4.00

The actual difference in the amount of fertilizers used is even greater than appears from a comparison of the "cost per farm," since the farms in the North are smaller than in the South. The cultivation of cigar leaf in

[1] *Cf. U. S. Census, 1900, Agriculture, Part II*, p. 509.

Northern States is often classed, not without reason, with truck-gardening rather than with ordinary farming.

Along with the tendency toward intensive cultivation on small farms, has come a diversification of crops. This has been furthered by several factors: the hazardous character of the crop, over-production, and intensive cultivation which has made possible a larger crop on a smaller area. In the North, where the tobacco farms are situated near cities, truck-gardening is profitable as a by-industry. In the South the tenant usually raises food products—corn, wheat, vegetables, meat—for private consumption. As was stated previously, only 34 per cent of the 300,000 farms reporting tobacco derive more than 40 per cent of their income from this single crop.[1] What a small portion of each farm is devoted to tobacco cultivation may be seen from the following figures:[2]

FARM AREA DEVOTED TO THE CULTIVATION OF TOBACCO.

Size of farms reporting tobacco. Acres.	Acres per farm reporting tobacco. South Atlantic Division.	South Central Division.
3 and under 10	1.3	2.2
10 and under 20	2.3	2.8
20 and under 50	2.9	2.9
50 and under 100	3.3	3.0
100 and under 175	4.2	3.5
175 and under 260	5.3	4.9
260 and under 500	6.6	7.1
500 and under 1000	8.5	11.2
1000 and over	12.3	19.1

As has already been stated labor plays a very important rôle in the cultivation of tobacco. It is not only quantity but a superior quality of labor that is required in pro-

[1] Where tobacco farms are leased out on the crop-sharing system provision is made usually for the cultivation of crops other than tobacco.

[2] *Cf. Twelfth Census, Agriculture, Part II*, p. 510.

ducing leaf tobacco. In the Northern States production is carried on usually by the farm owners who employ help during the summer months. Only about fifty per cent of the Southern leaf is produced directly by owners of land. Over thirty per cent of the farms are cultivated by share tenants. There are several forms of land tenure; the most common being that in which the owner leases to the tenant a specified area, supplies him with the necessary farm implements, work-animals, barns, one-half of the fertilizers, etc., and receives one-half of the crop harvested.[1] It is only where the owner advances most of the capital and land and the tenant contributes merely his own labor and one-half of the cost of fertilizers that the product is divided equally between the owner and the tenant. The tenant's share naturally increases in proportion as he contributes more capital in addition to his own labor; in which instance the lease usually calls for a three-fourth share to the tenant and one-fourth to the owner. The lease also usually stipulates the conditions under which crops other than that of tobacco are to be cultivated; the division of these secondary crops, between the tenant and the owner, is the same as that for tobacco.

The question as to which system of tenure and labor yields the best results is complicated by the fact that a slight variation in the character of the soil, or in the capital improvements, affects the final productivity. The product attributed to each of the several factors is difficult to single out. From figures compiled from the

[1] In Virginia the owner supplies not only the necessary land, dwelling and farm implements, but barns for curing, work animals, and feed for animals. He also pays taxes on the land, and contributes one-half the cost of fertilizers as well as one-half the cost of marketing the tobacco. The net return is divided equally.

twelfth census,[1] it appears that in the South the yield in quantity of leaf tobacco per acre under the crop-sharing system is as high as under the system of direct ownership. Even in the Northern States, Connecticut, Pennsylvania and Ohio, the same holds true, though the share-tenant system is less common. Where the cash-tenant system prevails the yield is often equally favorable, for instance, in Maryland, Pennsylvania, and Kentucky. In other states, however, the cash-tenant system is not so productive.[2] The table on the next page indicates the relation between the various forms of tenure, the extent to which each prevails, and their corresponding productivity in eight leading tobacco states.

From this table it appears that only fifty per cent of the tobacco-raising farms in the South are operated directly by the owners, and over thirty per cent by share-tenants. What is more surprising is that less than sixty per cent of the tobacco acreage in the North Atlantic and North Central States is cultivated by their owners directly, and fully thirty per cent of the acreage is operated by share-tenants.[3]

It is difficult to determine from a social standpoint, whether cultivation by tenants is less productive than under direct and partial ownership. The general consensus of opinion is that the quality of the leaf, as well as the final character of the land improvements, is apt to be better where the land is worked by its owner than by a tenant. The yield per acre of the former generally equals that of the latter. It is, however, not a conclu-

[1] *U. S. Census, 1900, Agriculture, Part II*, pp. 530–531.

[2] In the South whenever the landlord loses all interest in farming but cannot dispose of his land he usually tries to rent his land on the "cash tenant" basis.

[3] *Cf. U. S. Census, Agriculture, Part II*, pp. 530–531.

Number of Farms of Specified Tenure, with Yield per Acre. 1900.

	Total number of farms.	Yield per acre lbs.	Owners.		Share tenants.		Cash tenants.		Part owners.		Owners and tenants.		Managers.	
			Per cent of total farms.	Yield per acre lbs.	Per cent of total farms.	Yield per acre lbs.	Per cent of total farms.	Yield per acre lbs.	Per cent of total farms.	Yield per acre lbs.	Per cent of total farms.	Yield per acre lbs.	Per cent of total farms.	Yield per acre lbs.
United States ..	308,317	788	54	808	28	756	8	763	6	787	1.5	835	.3	800
Kentucky	86,594	817	56	812	27	817	6	840	6	850	2	810	.5	825
North Carolina .	51,106	628	46	623	37	625	7.7	625	6	605	1	585	.3	750
Virginia........	44,872	667	50	700	32	625	10	615	5	667	1.2	740	.8	667
Ohio	16,666	923	50	900	35	925	4	800	7	943	2	965	.5	850
Tennessee	29,960	684	56	690	25	615	8	650	7	650	2	775	.6	730
Wisconsin......	6,916	1345	61	1380	21	1300	9	1230	4	1230	1.5	1400	.6	1335
Pennsylvania ...	9,621	1495	60	1400	25	1500	9	1480	2	1650	.4	1450	1	1500
Maryland	5,338	573	48	525	40	550	5	630	3	525	.4	550	1	625
Connecticut	2,909	1673	73	1680	8	1700	6	1650	7	1590	3	1660	.9	1520

sive test to compare the *quantity* produced by all forms in general at any particular time and in a particular place. The relative productiveness of two systems of tenure can be measured absolutely only where the specific farm is cultivated by the same kind of labor with the same amount of capital, under the two different systems of tenure. It is, for instance, impossible to learn from the census data the difference in the natural fertility of the soil cultivated respectively by "owners" and "tenants." It is just this variation, however, in the natural fertility that may be responsible for the difference in the yield per acre. Likewise with the other factors in production, labor and capital. Moreover the weight of the crop is no indication of the net productivity since the quality of the leaf produced is a large factor in determining its price. So also the improvements on the land must be considered as an asset in measuring the relative merits of the two systems.

A similar difficulty presents itself in attempting to compare the efficiency of "white" and "colored" labor. The figures, however, point too much in one direction for doubting the superiority of the former. For under no system of tenure and in no section of the country do the farms of the "colored" labor yield per acre as much as the farms of the "white" labor. The table[1] on the next page has been compiled to show this apparent difference in efficiency between the two kinds of labor.

It is worth noting that the highest yield per acre is obtained by colored labor where "managers" are engaged, the inference being that the negro works best under the spur of a taskmaster. It is surprising to discover that among colored laborers, "owners" produce

[1] *Cf. U. S. Census, Agriculture, Part II*, pp. 511–512.

YIELD PER ACRE BY CENSUS DIVISIONS.

	Farms of White Farmers.	Farms of Colored Farmers.
	Pounds per acre.	Pounds per acre.
United States	814	615
North Atlantic Division	1490	1119
North Central Division	1023	834
South Atlantic Division	661	584
South Central Division	800	690

YIELD PER ACRE FOR WHITE AND COLORED FARMERS UNDER VARIOUS TENURES IN UNITED STATES.

Farms Classified by Tenure.	White Farmers.	Colored Farmers.
	Pounds per acre.	Pounds per acre.
All farms	814	615
Owners	822	595
Part owners	812	617
Owners and tenants	843	178
Managers	807	667
Cash tenants	805	596
Share tenants	797	627

less than "tenants." We should naturally expect the reverse to be true on the assumption that only the most efficient negroes become "owners" of land. The seeming anomaly is partly explained by the fact that the negroes have been able to purchase only a poorer grade of land, besides being embarrassed by a lack of capital necessary for farm improvements.[1]

Introductory to our discussion of some of the interesting developments in the production of leaf since the Civil War, we append statistics presenting the distribution of the tobacco crop with the percentage for each leading state; while the table on the next page shows the actual weight of the crops.[2]

PERCENTAGE OF TOTAL PRODUCTION FOR THE ELEVEN LEADING STATES (1860–1905).

	1860.	1870.	1880.	1890.	1900.	1905.
Total for 11 States	88.1	87.2	91.9	93.0	95.7	99.2
Kentucky	24.9	40.0	36.2	45.4	36.2	36.2
North Carolina	7.5	4.2	5.7	7.4	14.6	13.1
Virginia	28.5	14.1	16.9	9.9	14.1	12.6
Ohio	5.7	7.1	7.3	7.7	7.5	7.9
Tennessee	10.0	8.1	6.2	7.4	5.6	5.0
Wisconsin	0.02	0.3	2.0	3.9	5.2	8.5
Pennsylvania	0.2	1.3	7.8	5.9	4.8	3.3
Maryland	8.8	6.0	5.6	2.5	2.8	3.1
South Carolina	0.02	0.01	0.01	0.04	2.2	1.5
Connecticut	1.6	3.5	3.1	1.8	2.0	3.7
Massachusetts	.8	2.5	1.0	.6	.7	1.3

The figures indicate a heavy diminution in the decade following the Civil War, particularly in States like Vir-

[1] The writer is indebted to Mr. L. S. Thomas, Martinsville, Va., for some of the information concerning the cultivation of tobacco and concerning existing economic conditions in Virginia.

[2] Compiled from *U. S. Census, Agriculture, Part II*, pp. 528–29, and *Year-books of Department of Agriculture*.

PRODUCTION OF "LEAF" FROM 1860-1905 FOR 13 LEADING STATES.

	1860. Pounds.	1870. Pounds.	1880. Pounds.	1890. Pounds.	1900. Pounds.	1905. Pounds.
United States total	434,209,461	262,735,341	472,661,157	488,256,646	868,163,275	633,033,719
Kentucky	108,126,840	105,305,869	171,120,784	221,880,303	314,288,050	238,975,000
North Carolina	32,853,250	11,150,087	26,986,213	36,375,258	127,503,400	83,156,000
Virginia	123,968,312	37,086,364	79,988,868	48,522,655	122,884,900	79,952,000
Ohio	25,092,581	18,741,973	34,735,235	37,853,563	65,957,100	50,000,000
Tennessee	43,448,097	21,465,452	29,365,052	36,368,395	49,157,550	31,874,000
Wisconsin	87,340	960,813	10,608,423	19,389,166	45,500,480	53,833,000
Pennsylvania	3,181,586	3,467,539	36,943,272	28,956,247	41,502,620	20,994,000
Maryland	38,410,965	15,785,339	26,082,147	12,356,838	24,589,480	19,393,000
South Carolina	104,412	34,805	45,678	222,898	19,895,970	9,254,000
Connecticut	6,000,133	8,328,798	14,044,652	8,874,924	16,930,770	23,011,500
Massachusetts	3,232,867	7,313,202	4,369,338	2,785,076	6,406,230	8,302,000
Missouri	25,086,196	12,320,483	12,015,657	9,424,823	3,041,996	1,295,000
Illinois	6,885,262	5,249,274	3,935,825	3,042,936	1,447,150	1,018,800

ginia, North Carolina, Missouri, which suffered most from the economic disturbances and financial embarassments attending the rebellion. Since 1870, however, our production has kept pace with the increasing domestic and foreign consumption of tobacco. During the last decade (1895-1905) our annual production approximated 700,000,000 lbs., which is about thirty-five per cent of the entire crop of that part of the world for which there are reliable statistics.[1] Nearly one-half of our crop is exported.

Of our entire crop, twenty per cent is cigar leaf and eighty per cent "manufacturing" leaf (used in plug, smoking and chewing tobacco, cigarettes and snuff.) As indicated above, the cigar leaf is produced in Wisconsin, Connecticut, Massachusetts, Pennsylvania, New York, Florida and part of Ohio. The "manufacturing" leaf (80 per cent of our total crop) is confined to our Southern States, principally Kentucky, North Carolina, Virginia, Tennessee and Maryland. The combined product of the first three is alone sixty-two per cent of the total production and about ninety per cent of the entire Southern crop.

Since the Civil War there have been some interesting movements in the shifting of the centres of production. Virginia, which for nearly two and a half centuries was the leading tobacco section in the country, surrendered its supremacy to Kentucky, and has since been surpassed by North Carolina. This is explained by several causes. First the collapse of slavery affected Virginia planters more severely than those of other states; there were in Virginia twice as many slaves as in Kentucky. A

[1] The world-crop is estimated at 2,333,000,000 lbs. *Cf. Year-book of the Department of Agriculture*, 1905, pp. 714-717.

comparison of the size of tobacco plantations and the number of slaves engaged in production, prior to the War in Virginia, North Carolina, and Kentucky reveals the relative extent to which the destruction of the old system of production affected the industry in these states. This is shown in the following table:

SLAVE LABOR IN 1860.[1]

States.	Total number of slaves.	Number of slaves on plantations holding 10 or more slaves.	Number of holders in 10 leading tobacco counties.	Slaves per holder in 10 same counties.
Virginia	490,865	280,190	1028	11
North Carolina	331,059	205,885	580	9
Kentucky	225,483	129,390	665	7

The inability to command the necessary labor, after the war, was aggravated by the loss of capital during the struggle, which left many of the Virginia planters in a helpless condition. In addition to these factors (the loss of slave labor and the destruction of capital) must be mentioned an equally important influence detrimental to Virginia's position as a tobacco producer, namely, the impoverishment of the soil. Both Washington and Jefferson had foreseen that Virginia's land was being worked too hard by tobacco planters. The full realization of this fact came with the opening up of the virgin soil of

[1] *Cf. U. S. Census, 1860, Agriculture.* Compare, with respect to acreage per plantation and number of slaves per plantation, the principal tobacco counties in Virginia and Kentucky. In Virginia—Albemarle, Bedford, Dinwiddi, Halifax, Louisa, Lunenberg, Pittsylvania, Mecklenberg, Brunswick and Buckingham. In Kentucky—Union, Warren, Todd, Trigg, Logan, Christian, Dorris, Graves, Henderson and Hopkins. In North Carolina—Alamance, Granville, Warren, Caswell, Rockingham, Person, Orange, Stokes and Forsyth.

Kentucky and Tennessee, as well as of a new region in North Carolina well adapted to the cultivation of tobacco. The fresh soil of Kentucky, Tennessee and North Carolina for some time enabled the planters in these states to undersell Virginia growers. Recently the introduction of cheap commercial fertilizers has enabled Virginia landowners partially to rehabilitate the soil and to increase production.

Another interesting movement has been the retrogression in the cultivation of tobacco in Maryland, Missouri and Illinois. The rapid industrial growth in these states rendered the tobacco lands more valuable for residential purposes and urban truck-gardening. The process of substitution was especially active in Maryland (Anne, Arundel and Prince George counties). The combined product of these two counties in 1860 was 20,000,000 pounds and in 1900 less than 10,000,000 pounds. The same development took place in Howard and Chariton counties, Missouri, and in Johnson, Saline and Williamson counties, Illinois. The most striking example, however, of crop substitution occurred in Kentucky, where large parts of the famous "blue-grass," stock-raising section has been transformed into tobacco farms. In the South there is frequently a mutual substitution of tobacco and cotton crops depending upon the prospective market price of each. This is notably true in North Carolina and in the Piedmont region generally. One important consequence of the rapid expansion of tobacco cultivation in Kentucky, North Carolina and Tennessee has been the shifting of the manufacturing centres westward from Virginia towns to St. Louis, Louisville, Cincinnati, and Durham, North Carolina.

We pass at this point to the consideration of a problem which is at present of vital importance to the planter, the marketing of leaf. As we shall see presently, the discontent and unrest among Southern growers have their origin in the undue advantage possessed by the Tobacco Trust in purchasing its leaf. A complete appreciation of this situation depends upon an understanding of the external organization of the market; the means whereby sellers and buyers are brought together. The method of marketing cigar leaf differs from the marketing of Southern leaf. It is to the latter that we shall first direct our attention.

Every important tobacco section has its public warehouse, situated in the nearest town or city. There, on appointed days, the grower conveys his crop, which, after being exhibited to the buyer for inspection, is publicly auctioned to the highest bidder. The leaf may be sold either "loose," as in the "heavy shipping" districts, or "inspected" (a method common to all districts). In the former case ("loose" marketing), the leaf is sold in the bulk without being sampled or inspected, as is the procedure in the latter case. The method of "inspection" is scientific; warehouse officials, under bond, draw samples from each lot or crop, grade and mark them. To each sample is attached a note or tag bearing the name of the warehouse, the seller, the warehouse number, the gross weight of the crop or lot, the date of inspection and the inspector's name. The warehouse is under supervision of the State law and is responsible for losses traceable to fraudulent practices of the warehouse officials. On the basis of these samples, the lots or crops they represent are auctioned off, by warehouse officials, to the highest bidder. In this case the buyer depends upon the accuracy and good judgment of the sampler in grading and prizing the leaf. If the price is not satisfactory the seller can withhold his wares. Each type of tobacco has its special market or markets; for instance, the "heavy shipping tobacco" of western Kentucky and Tennessee is sold largely at Louisville, Cincinnati and Clarksville. Almost the entire crop of Maryland and eastern Ohio is sent to markets at Baltimore. Durham and Winston are the large markets for the "yellow" tobacco of North Carolina; Richmond is the centre for all types of Virginia leaf. Burley leaf of Kentucky is shipped to points on the Ohio, principally Cincinnati.

The expense or cost of distribution which this warehouse system entails is very high. When sold "loose" the grower pays fifteen cents for having a load weighed, twenty-five cents for having it auctioned (each pile), besides paying a two and one-half per cent commission to the warehouse. Under the system of "inspection," there is first a storage charge ($1.50) per hogshead, an inspection and sampling fee (about $1.00 per hogshead), an insurance fee averaging one-half of one per cent of its value, an auction fee (twenty-five cents per sample) and a commission to the warehouse of about three per cent of selling value. The average marketing charges, including freight, drayage, warehouse inspection, auction fees, commission (three per cent), insurance (one-half of one per cent), are estimated at about ten per cent of the gross selling price. The charges traceable exclusively to the warehouse system of marketing, as such, that is, inspection fees, auction fees, commission fees, etc., are about five per cent of the selling price.[1]

To confer upon the planter the advantages that accrue to the seller from open competition among the buyers was the sole purpose and justification for this warehouse

[1] *Cf.* "The Distribution of the Tobacco Crop" in the *Report of the Industrial Commission*, 1900, vol. vi, pp. 307–321.

system. On the other hand the buyer was willing to pay a trifle more in return for the convenience and benefits derived from such a centralized public market. The original purpose of the plan, however, is vitiated and its advantages nullified just as soon as the buyers agree to pool their interests and depress prices by curtailing the very competition which the warehouse market sought to invite. It is to this condition that the Southern leaf market has come since the Tobacco Trust has secured control of from seventy-five to ninety per cent of the home market, especially in the sale of cigarettes, plug, and chewing tobacco. We must remember further that several large European countries (for instance France, Austria, Spain and Italy) exercise a monopoly over tobacco, and their purchases are made through single government agents. The complaint is made, with some degree of plausibility, that the Trust and these "Régie" agents have come to some secret understanding and parcelled out the markets among themselves, agreeing not to compete with one another.[1] Where two parties buy in the same market, a certain maximum price is fixed arbitrarily.

Such accusations are, of course, difficult to substantiate.[2] One fact, however, has become more and more obvious, namely, that in proportion as the Trust has extended its power over the market, prices of leaf have fallen. By 1896 the American Tobacco Company had succeeded in capturing the cigarette market. In that year leaf at Winston, N. C., the largest cigarette centre,

[1] *Cf.* Congressman Stanley's arraignment of the Trust in *Congressional Record*, June 2, 1906, p. 7923.

[2] Congressman Mudd of Maryland, in the interest of the growers of his State, recently introduced a bill calling for an investigation of "foreign tobacco monopolies."

brought six cents per lb., whereas in 1890 it sold for twelve cents, as shown in the following table:[1]

PRICE OF LEAF TOBACCO, WINSTON, N. C. (1889-1896).

	Cents per pound.		Cents per pound.
1889	12.3	1893	6.3
1890	11.8	1894	7.0
1891	9.1	1895	6.0
1892	8.6	1896	6.3

The crisis of 1893 was only partially responsible for this sharp decline in prices; for notwithstanding the development in the cigarette industry since 1896, prices of leaf used in its manufacture have never been as high as they were prior to the culmination of the Trust control in the early nineties. Similarly, when the plug interests were combined and controlled by the Continental Tobacco Company and the American Tobacco Company in the later part of the nineties, burley leaf suffered a decline. In the period from 1899 to 1904 Burley leaf (used in the manufacture of plug) averaged at Louisville and Cincinnati seven and one-half cents per lb., whereas it formerly marketed for ten cents. Since 1900 North Carolina "Brights" (used in smoking tobacco and cigarettes) brought only from six to eight cents per lb. at Winston, Durham and Danville markets compared with its former price of nine and ten cents. At Hopkinsville, Kentucky and Clarksville, Tennessee, large western markets, prices have dropped from eight and one-half cents in 1900 to seven cents in 1905. Nor must it be forgotten that during this period of declining prices of leaf, the planter was forced to pay increased prices not only for material and

[1] *Cf. Report of Industrial Commission*, 1900, vol. vi, p. 321.

labor employed in cultivation but also for commodities for private consumption.[1]

Despite all denials to the contrary, the blame for this price-depression has been placed by planters, with unanimous accord, at the door of the Trust. As a countermove, the growers have organized associations to force up prices either by curtailing the supply of leaf or by fixing an arbitrary price below which no sales are to be made. The most important of these associations, at the present time, are the following: the "Dark Tobacco Growers Association of Kentucky," the "Dark Tobacco Growers Association of Tennessee," the "Burley Tobacco Growers Association of Kentucky," the "Mutual Protective Association of Bright Tobacco Growers of Virginia and North Carolina," and the "Maryland Tobacco Growers Association." This mere enumeration indicates the extent to which, geographically at least, the Trust influence has made itself felt. Two obstacles stand in the way of an efficient concerted action among the farmers: one, the mere number and wide geographical distribution of planters with a lack of easy communication between them; the other, more important, difficulty is the financial inability to guarantee the small farmer the final disposal of his crop at a profitable price. Without this latter assurance the small farmer is reluctant to pledge or bind himself legally to the rules and action of the association; and without a legally enforceable contract there is nothing to prevent the individual farmer from selling his crop at a lower price in anticipation of a great slump, thus breaking the sellers' pool. One thing is certain,

[1] The prices quoted above (1896–1906) are taken from *The Western Tobacco Journal* and *The Tobacco Leaf*. For prices prior to 1896, *Cf.* Killebrew and Myrick, *The Tobacco Leaf*, pp. 487, 492, which prices are based on quotations of *The Western Tobacco Journal*.

namely, that the combination or union of over 200,000 planters must necessarily be less efficient than the centralized power of a Trust purchasing alone from seventy-five to ninety per cent of the entire crop consumed in this country. As a partial escape from the clutches of the Trust the growers are demanding a reform in the laws of the Internal Revenue system which would permit them to sell their leaf directly to consumers without paying the tax imposed at present on all forms of tobacco sold to consumers.[1]

We have thus far confined our discussion to the marketing of Southern leaf, its method and its problems. In the North there are no public warehouses where buyers and sellers can be brought together in open competition. In the first place, the leaf is not purchased, as is the Southern leaf, directly by the manufacturer, but by "packers." The latter, or their agents, visit the individual grower and bargain on the basis of the rough knowledge of the general market that each may happen to possess. The buyer usually has the advantage since his knowledge of the market is apt to be based on broader and more opportune insight into the conditions of the market in general. It is a wasteful system because it necessitates traveling expenses on the part of several buyers in search often of a doubtful seller. A saner method is the Southern warehouse system. In order to take advantage of the chaotic market, "packers" engage buyers residing in the tobacco-growing region. The "packer" often buys the entire crop, sometimes before it is ever harvested; he grades, sorts and "sweats" it in his own warehouse. The leaf jobber and large cigar

[1] *Cf. House Bill*, no. 14972, "An Act for the relief of Tobacco Farmers." There is little hope of this measure becoming a law.

manufacturer purchase from the packer; the leaf jobber in turn sells to the small manufacturer. The fact that strikes one in the organization of the distributing agencies is the existence of these many middlemen through whom leaf passes before it reaches the small, and often the large, cigar manufacturer. The price to the manufacturer, in case the leaf passes through the hands of packer and the jobber, is from forty to eighty per cent in advance of the original farm price paid to the grower. This margin of profit is altogether out of proportion to the services rendered, and exists only because of the vast number of small manufacturers who have not sufficient capital to buy directly from the grower. Once the Tobacco Trust is in possession of the cigar market (and the time is not far off),[1] both the packer and jobber will be forced to the wall.

The present high price of all classes of cigar leaf is partly the result of the Trust movement to eliminate the small manufacturer by making it unprofitable for him to continue in business. With an increase in the price of raw material the independent manufacturer is compelled to raise prices on the finished product. But the Trust continues to market its cigars at the old price in order to capture the trade, which is equivalent to underselling. In the meantime the farmer is enjoying high prices. Another factor, however, should not be overlooked in explaining the present high price of cigar leaf, namely, the tremendous growth of the cigar industry in the last ten years, which necessitated a supply of leaf not antici-

[1] Even as we write, the *New York Times* reports the absorption, by the Trust of the largest producers of domestic cigars, namely, the United Cigar Manufacturers' Co., having an annual output of 400,000,-000 cigars or about six per cent of the total output of the United States. The report has, however, been denied by the independent company.

pated by the grower. As a consequence we have had under-production for several years. Although "average" prices of cigar leaf are not always a safe guide, the following table does represent fairly the general tendency of the leaf market since 1900:

AVERAGE FARM PRICE OF CIGAR LEAF (1900–1905).[1]

	1900.	1901.	1902.	1903.	1904.	1905.
Connecticut	15	15	16	15	22	17
Massachusetts	15	12	15	12	18	16
New York............	8	7	8	8	10	10
Pennsylvania	6	6	6	7	8	10
Ohio	7	7	7	7	8	8
Wisconsin...........	7	8	7	6	7	10

This abnormally high price of leaf in the last few years has encouraged the free-trade agitators in their demands for a reduction of the high protective duties on cigar leaf. The home growers, however, were able to exercise sufficient political influence to prevent the passage of the "Payne Bill" which would have admitted the Philippine leaf, a cigar filler, at twenty-five per cent of the present tariff rate.[2]

Owing to the variety as well as the nature of the problems discussed, it is difficult to summarize the contents of this chapter. For the purpose of showing the hazardous character of the crop, as well as some of the larger problems in production, we began with a general description of some of the principal processes in the cultivation of tobacco. Since the abolition of slavery, the South has been confronted with a scarcity in the supply of efficient labor. With the collapse of slavery and the

[1] *Cf. Yearbook of Agricultural Dept. U. S.*, 1905, pp. 714–717.

[2] The bill passed the House, but has never been reported by the Senate Committee in charge of the bill.

plantation system, the large estates were soon broken up into small farms, and though the process of disintegration is not yet completed, it is being hastened by an ever increasing "absentee landlordism." In the absence of sufficient supply of wage labor, a large portion of the Southern land is leased to tenants who work under the crop-sharing system. After making allowances for differences in the fertility of soil, and farm improvements, we concluded that negro labor on the whole was not as efficient as "white labor." It is not, however, production but the marketing of goods that is bringing sleepless nights to the Southern planter. The Trust has forced prices down to a no-profit level. Controlling as it does from seventy-five to ninety per cent of the market (with exception of cigar goods), the Trust is in a position to dictate prices to the growers. The Northern grower of cigar leaf is temporarily enjoying high prices and large profits; but for him also is rapidly approaching the day of reckoning with the Trust. Unless our National Government should take decisive action, or some unforseen event occur, to check the onward march of the Trust, we shall, in all likelihood, witness presently among the Northern growers a depression in the price of cigar leaf similar in effect to that experienced during the last decade by Southern growers.

CHAPTER III

THE MANUFACTURE OF TOBACCO

THE life history of any industry is largely determined by two forces, the technical conditions of production and the character of the selling market. Every transformation in the organization of an industry can be traced ultimately to some change either in the methods of production or in the methods of marketing the product. It is in this light that we interpret and explain the development of our present capitalistic system, in the progress of which competition has been the driving force. Intensified competition has in each instance been the result of, or necessitated by, some technical improvement within the industry, or some alteration in the world market. That the tobacco industry is no exception to this general rule will become apparent as we attempt to explain its development in terms of these two factors, conditions of production and the selling market.

With respect to conditions of production, we must distinguish between the manufacture of cigars and the manufacture of all other products—chewing and smoking tobacco, plug, snuff and cigarettes; the latter being machine-made, while the former are largely hand products. To this primary differentiation are due the many points of variation in the development of each branch of the industry.

Simple as are the steps, "bunch-making" and "rolling," in the making of a cigar, they have up to the present time, baffled the inventor seeking to reduce them to automatic machine processes. "Bunch-making" consists in the selection of "filler" leaf, placing it into a "binder" leaf and shaping it into the desired form. "Rolling" involves merely a cutting of the "wrapper" leaf and rolling it around the "bunch." Upon the skill, or lack of it, in "bunch-making" depends the smoking value of the cigar. The difficulty sometimes experienced by the smoker in "drawing" the smoke is often due to some imperfect twist in the filler; a common defect in cigars made by beginners. To the art of rolling is due the external appearance of the cigar, which is no small factor in determining its sale. This brief description will enable the reader to understand why this skill, involving as it does accurate judgment and artful manipulation in bunching and rolling, has been only partially displaced by the machine and the unskilled worker.

Up to 1870 labor, and not capital, was the all-important factor in the cigar industry. The only tools employed were a small hand-knife for cutting the wrapper, an inexpensive board upon which the wrapper could be cut and the cigar rolled, and a block of wood with a stationary knife attached, known as a "tuck-cutter," for measuring and cutting the finished cigar to the required size. In 1869 a wooden "mold" was introduced, which aided the bunch-makers in shaping the cigar (the "bunch"). Except in all hand-made cigars, the mold is still universally used. It is a very simple device: a wooden block (about 18 inches by 6 inches by 3 inches), comprised of an upper and lower half; to the lower half is attached a row of matrices, into which the fresh bunches are placed; to the upper half is attached a similar number of "cups," shaped to fit tightly over the corresponding matrices. The "block" or "mold," filled with cigars, is then put into an ordinary hand-lever press. The mold is not a machine, but simply a tool which facilitates the making of bunches. It made possible, however, a division of labor into bunch-makers and rollers. Prior to the introduction of the mold each cigarmaker did his own bunch-making and his own rolling as he still does to-day in all hand-made work.

The introduction of the mold, however, did not revolutionize the organization of production. It was too inexpensive to embarrass the small producer with little capital, and, besides, it did not make large-scale production more economical than before. The use of the mold, however, has made possible the employment of a less skilled grade of labor, since a cigar made by hand requires several years of practice, whereas a beginner can be taught to make mold cigars in one year, and less. The substitution of a less skilled grade of labor was, however, open to small and large producers alike.

A more radical improvement in production has come within the last decade, with the introduction of bunch-making machinery, by which a short scrap filler bunch is made entirely by automatic machinery. The scrap filler is placed into a hopper, which apportions the quantity necessary for each cigar, rolls the bunch, places it into a mold and presses it. Human labor being necessary only in feeding the machine and in spreading "binders," which can be performed by unskilled operators, usually young boys and girls. This invention has made possible a saving not only in the quantity but in the quality of human labor. The machine, representing an investment of $350, with an operator receiving $5.00 a week, can produce 25,000 bunches per week, which, if done with molds (non-machine) would cost $75. Here is a tremendous saving in the cost of production by machine as compared with hand and mold labor. These bunching machines, however, are employed only in the production of cheap, short-filler cigars, in which the filler is first cut up into small flakes or "scraps." In the manufacture of these cigars no selection of filler leaf is necessary, as is the case in the ordinary long-filler cigar. As the largest proportion of our domestic cigars retailing at five cents and upward are made of long filler, most of our cigars are still made by a combination of hand and mold work; and a smaller proportion, scrap goods, are made by machine.

In addition to the bunching machine there is the suction tool (not a machine), which enables the roller to cut the wrappers with greater accuracy. By means of air pressure the wrapper leaf is drawn tightly over a perforated plate of the desired shape for rolling purposes; a small, circular knife is then guided by hand around a fixed track or groove on the plate. As this tool does not dispense with the skill and judgment necessary in placing the leaf, ready for cutting and rolling, its economic utility is still doubtful. To take advantage of the slight gain made in cutting after a pattern, large factories resort to a division of labor between cutters and rollers, since inexperienced and cheap labor can be employed in cutting the leaf. Machine production is, however, fast gaining ground and is responsible for the increased rate of concentration within the last ten years (1895–1905).

As a result of these methods of production, wherein hand labor has played a more important rôle than capital, the industry has been organized largely on the domestic (household) plan, and in large cities under the small sweat-shop system. The skilled worker, with a mere pittance of capital, can engage in business as an independent producer, relying on a local patronage for the sale of his goods. As a consequence, the personal equation has been an active influence in determining the character of the industry. The entire market of a city or town is divided among many producers, each capitalizing, as it were, the trade dependent on his direct acquaintance and personal influence either with the retailer or with the consumer, and often with both. This local character of the selling market is further intensified by the opportunity offered to various petty retail stands—in barber shops, grocery stores, hotels, saloons—to profit by transient patronage, or a traffic of convenience. Although originally a resultant of the conditions of production, this local market reacts in turn to impede any movement toward concentration, the latter depending upon an impersonal extensive market. The Tobacco Trust, seeing in this traditional character of the market an obstacle in its path, is attempting to break down the local market or to overcome it by organizing its own retail agencies—the United Cigar Stores.

Turning to statistics, we are not surprised to find that the cigar industry is still in many hands. As late as 1895, twenty years after the introduction of the mold, there were no signs of a decided breaking down of the domestic system of production. It is only in the last decade (1895–1905) that there has been a marked tendency toward concentration in the large factories and a disappearance of the smaller ones. The following table represents the number of establishments and output since 1875:

[1] Based on annual *Reports of Commissioner of Internal Revenue.*

AVERAGE OUTPUT OF CIGARS PER ESTABLISHMENT.

	Number of establishments.	Total output per factory per year.	Percent increase per establishment.
1875	15,005	130,000	
1895	30,000	145,000	10
1905	26,700	290,000	100

As the maximum number of cigar makers in the country in 1895 was probably about 120,000, the average shop or factory would then be employing only four workers. Putting the maximum in 1905 at 150,000, the average would still be only six. Averages here are misleading. The actual situation presents on the one hand shops of one or two employees (including the owner), and on the other hand, large factories employing as many as one thousand workers.

In order to present more accurately the real character of the organization on the side of production, we give in the following table statistics for Pennsylvania, the leading cigar manufacturing state in the Union:

ORGANIZATION OF THE CIGAR INDUSTRY IN PENNSYLVANIA.

	Number of establishments.	Capital invested.	Employees.	Value of product.
1890	1967	$9,471,276	17,385	$19,978,000
1900	2664	13,836,368	25,045	31,483,141
1905	2774	22,082,487	30,320	39,079,966

Notwithstanding the fact that the above census figures include all factories having an output of $500 or more, the total (2774) is only fifty per cent of the entire number reported by the Commissioner of Internal Revenue.[1] Even of those reported in the U. S. Census[2] (as given above) the average number of employees per establish-

[1] *Cf. Report of Commissioner of Internal Revenue* ending June, 1906.

[2] *Census of Manufactures, Bulletin* 60.

ment in 1890 was nine; in 1900, less than 10; and in 1905, only 11. The output per factory was only $10,000 in 1890; $11,000 in 1900, and $15,000 in 1905. The movement toward concentration, stimulated by machine production, was greatest in the last five years. In Pennsylvania, for instance, where the domestic system has persisted with greatest vigor, seventy-eight establishments, less than three per cent of the total number (2774) produced fifty-four per cent of the entire product in 1905,[1] whereas, sixty-eight per cent of the establishments (1908) produced less than ten per cent of the entire product. In the following table is shown the distribution of output in small shops and large factories:

SUMMARY OF ESTABLISHMENTS FOR PENNSYLVANIA CIGARS AND CIGARETTES.[2]

	Establishments.		Wage earners.		Value of product.	
Producing	No.	%	No.	%	Amount.	%
Less than $5,000....	1908	68.8	2,600	8.6	$3,589,682	9.2
$5,000-20,000	588	21.2	5,018	16.5	5,615,226	14.4
$20,000-100,000	200	7.2	6,886	22.7	8,761,972	22.4
$100,000 and more.	78	2.8	15,816	52.2	21,112,242	54.0

From this it appears that only nine per cent of the total number employed work in factories of two men or less; and over 62 per cent are engaged in establishments averaging 200. What is true of Pennsylvania is true generally of the other states. In New York State, for instance, 72 per cent of all the cigar and cigarette establishments[3] manufacture only eight per cent of the product. In Ohio 75 per cent of the establishments produced, in 1905, only 14 per cent of the product, whereas 6.8 per cent produced 67 per cent of the pro-

[1] *Census of Manufactures Bulletin*, 60, p. 40.

[2] As Pennsylvania produces scarcely any cigarettes, the figures are practically for cigars.

[3] *Cf. Census of Manufactures*, 1905, N. Y. *Bulletin*, 59.

duct. In Massachusetts 60 per cent of the factories produced 6.6 per cent, and 12 per cent of the factories produced 80 per cent of the total product. Making allowance for the output in the many small shops not reported in the census, it is safe to assume that less than twenty-five per cent of the total product of the country is manufactured in small shops of two or three workers, which were almost universal up to 1880, and very extensive up to 1890. Gradually but surely the large factory is crowding out the small shop.

Machine production is not the only factor making for concentration in the cigar industry. To this must be added the desire to economize by purchasing raw material on a large scale, not only the leaf, but boxes and labels. Furthermore, there is the decided gain in advertising and marketing expenses which, in the cigar trade, is no small item, since the value of a cigar depends so largely on a supposed reputation created by such advertisement. The many large factories existing prior to the introduction of machinery owe their position to their economies in the purchase of raw material, the cost of advertising and the expense of selling agents. It was these large factories that first encroached upon the market of the local producers, since the former found it necessary, as well as profitable, to extend their markets.

The largest cigar factories are located either near the tobacco fields or in proximity to a world labor market and are found in New York, Philadelphia, Boston, Chicago and Cincinnati. The important factories at Tampa and Key West are located there to be near the source of supply of raw material,[1] Cuba and Florida, and

[1] It has been charged that many of the manufacturers moved to Florida because of the possible advantage in buying cheap leaf tobacco smuggled from Cuba.

also to take advantage of Spanish-Cuban labor, which can be more easily induced to settle in those cities.

The following table gives the distribution of cigar manufactures among the leading states in this country:

PRODUCTION OF CIGARS SINCE 1880.

	1880. %	1885. %	1890. %	1895. %	1900. %	1905. %	Largest manufacturing center.
Pennsylvania	19	23	27	28	26	28	Philadelphia.
New York	32	33	27	23	21	20	New York.
Ohio	9	7	7	10	10	8.8	Cincinnati.
Illinois	5	4	5	6	4	4	Chicago.
Maryland	...	...	...	...	6	6	Baltimore.
Virginia	...	...	...	...	5	8	Richmond.
Florida	...	...	4	3	4	4	Tampa.

The lead taken by Pennsylvania has been due to the profitable exploitation of child and female labor under the household system of production. A large quantity of cheap cigars and stogies is still made in this way in the homes of farmers during the winter months, and in the homes of the mine workers throughout the entire year. Cigars are thus produced at fifty per cent below the average non-union wage.

As a result of the economic waste involved in the disorganized character of the retail trade, the rate of profit on each unit sold must necessarily be high. When a business is apportioned among so many hands as is the cigar trade, large profits must be offered to the retailer as an inducement to carry in stock that particular line of goods. The cigar that is ordinarily retailed for five cents ($50 per M.) is bought from the manufacturer or jobber for $25 and $30 per thousand, the cost of production approximating $20 per thousand; so that the manufacturer's profit is 20 per cent and the retailer's 100 per cent. It is the elimination of this unusually high rate of middleman's profit that the Trust aims to accomplish through the organization of its chain of up-to-date retail stores. By this development the Tobacco Trust is rendered complete in its organization from the purchase of the raw leaf to the sale of the finished product direct to the consumer. In our opinion, there is a distinct gain to the general consuming public through the concentrated organization of the cigar industry, provided the Trust is not in a position to enjoy a monopoly profit as a result of its position. A successful control of the selling market will mean a forward step in the direction of concentration on the side of production. For it is the trade of the small store and the small manufacturer that is being captured, and this will hence involve merely an addition to the working capacity of the large stores and larger factories.

Thus both factors seem to react upon each other in shaping the character of the industry: on the one side, every important change in methods of production has led to concentration, which, in turn, has made possible, because profitable, an extension of the market; and, on the other hand, every successful expansion of the retail market has signified a concentration in production.

In the manufacture of plug, smoking and chewing tobacco, snuff and cigarettes, the course of development has been similar to that of the cigar industry only more rapid. The production of "manufactured tobacco,"[1] cigarettes and snuff, however, was never carried on to the same extent, under the domestic system nor was its sale restricted, as was that of cigars, to so limited a local

[1] "Manufactured tobacco" includes plug, chewing and pipe smoking tobacco, and fine cut. We have followed here the classification used in the reports of the Internal Revenue Commissioner—manufactured tobacco, snuff, cigars and cigarettes.

and personal market. In these branches of the industry machinery at an early date became more important than skilled labor, and later, even crude labor was largely displaced by improved machinery. To-day only five per cent of the total cost of production is attributable to labor, whereas in the cigar industry labor still represents about twenty per cent.

The reason for the adaptability of machinery to the production of manufactured tobacco, snuff, and cigarettes, is obvious enough when we consider the nature of the products. In the manufacture of plug, chewing tobacco, or cigarettes, no selection and shaping of the leaf is required. The leaf, before it enters into the finished product, is cut up into flakes or shreds, or, as in the manufacture of snuff, is pulverized by power machines. The finishing of the product consists merely in shaping the raw material into the desired form, which can also be easily performed by machinery. Perhaps a detailed description of some of the important processes in the manufacture of a single product, like plug, will make clear the general technical conditions of the entire industry. The leaf must first be stripped; that is, the tough midrib removed. For this a machine has been introduced. As the leaf in one bundle varies in quality, a selection and classification is necessary for the different purposes. This is done by unskilled female labor. The leaf is then subjected to adulteration. Large vats of "sauces" and "flavors," the principal ingredients in which are sugar, licorice and alcohol, are prepared, into which the leaf is dipped. After it is saturated with this flavoring sauce, the leaf is passed through rollers or wringers, which squeeze out the surplus liquid. The sweetened leaf is next taken to a "lumping" room, where a machine cuts, presses and shapes it into the conventional form.

Finally the sweetened cakes are wrapped in carefully selected and attractive leaf. There remains further only the pressing and packing into cases. In all these processes it will be observed that where human labor is necessary, it is of a low and unskilled grade, the heavy work being performed by machinery.

What is said of the manufacture of plug, is likewise true of the other products—smoking and chewing tobacco, snuff and cigarettes—in connection with all of which machinery is more important than skilled labor. It is worth noting that in the manufacture of cigars, machinery has been successfully introduced only in the production of that class of goods which is not unlike cigarettes, that is, "scrap" or short filler cigars. It is necessary for the machine merely to measure the quantity of leaf and to roll it, but not to select and shape the leaf, as in the manufacture of long filler cigars.

The possibility of employing machinery and crude labor was not the only factor which led to large scale production. An important item in the market value of manufactured tobacco, snuff and cigarettes, is the element of uniformity. Once the customer is accustomed to a brand he will continue to use it, provided the quality can be sustained from year to year. Now, in order to maintain this uniformity, the manufacturer must be in a position to purchase from year to year the same quality of raw leaf. The large producer, rather than the small one, possesses this power, the choice of the latter being usually limited to that part of the crop which has not been selected by the large producer. As a result of this, the small manufacturer may often pay less than the large manufacturer, but his goods lack uniformity.

Another condition of the trade which favors the large rather than the small producer, is the importance of advertising a brand. Notwithstanding the fact that each manufacturer uses a secret formula in the adulteration process, the products of one manufacturer are not fundamentally different in character or quality from those of his competitors. The sale of the finished commodity must accordingly be made on the basis of a created or fictitious reputation. Hence the value of advertising brands, which are always more economical when operated on a large scale.

Under such conditions the industry soon became organized on the basis of large-scale production. Improved and costly machinery, economy in the purchase of raw material in bulk, not only leaf, but adulterating ingredients, as well as labels and packing material, economy in advertising brands and in marketing goods, all have coöperated in favor of the large manufacturer as opposed to the small producer.

Although the output of manufactured tobacco in 1875 was far greater than that of cigars, there were only 980 tobacco manufacturers as compared with 15,000 cigar manufacturers. Subsequently each technical improvement enabled the large producer to increase his output at a less cost per unit, while he could easily dispose of his goods in the market which he had already organized and controlled. In 1860 and 1870 the average capital investment of a cigar factory was less than $3,000, (chiefly circulating capital), whereas the investment in a manufactured tobacco factory averaged $15,000 in 1860 and $25,000 in 1870. Concentration in production since the Civil War is shown in the following table, based on census figures:[1]

[1] The Census omitted smaller factories. The figures of the Internal Revenue reports show no such decline in the establishments as would appear from the Census data.

CONCENTRATION IN THE MANUFACTURE OF TOBACCO.

	1860.	1870.	1880.	1890.	1900.	1905.
Number of establishments.	626	573	477	395	437	433
Capital invested per establishments	$15,000	$25,000	$40,000	$75,000	$100,000	$400,000
Employees per establishment.	30	40	70	78	75	55
Output per establishment ..	$35,000	$70,000	$110,000	$165,000	$235,000	$270,000

Judged from the standpoint of capital investment as well as output per factory,[1] the above figures indicate a rapid concentration since 1890. A second inference from these data is the increasing importance of machinery in production. Although the value of the output from 1880 to 1903 increased from $52,000,000 to $116,000,000, (120 per cent increase), the number of workers engaged in the industry fell from thirty-two thousand to twenty-three thousand, (a decrease of 40 per cent). Anticipating here the Trust development, discussed in our following chapter, we desire to point out, in passing the extent to which large-scale production and concentration had been realized prior to the control of the industry by the American Tobacco Company in the nineties.

Parallel with the movement toward large-scale production has been a corresponding concentration in the localization of the industry. In 1905 more than 68 per cent of the total output came from eight cities—St. Louis, Durham and Winston (N. C.), Louisville, Richmond, Cincinnati, New York, Petersburg (Va.). The combined output of fifty factories in St. Louis, Louisville, Winston and Durham, was $63,000,000, or more than fifty per cent of the total product manufactured in the United

[1] We do not refer to concentration of control or ownership.

States. This geographical concentration has been hastened by the Trust ownership and control of seventy-five per cent of the entire industry.

The location of these large factories has been determined by two factors: nearness to supply of raw material and proximity to the labor market. In general, the South, which produces the leaf used in manufacturing, has the largest output. The large plug and smoking tobacco factories of St. Louis, Louisville and Cincinnati are supplied with Burley leaf from Kentucky, Tennessee and Ohio. Winston and Durham are located in the regions of North Carolina that grow the leaf used in the manufacture of cigarette and smoking tobacco. These locations are favorable also for the employment of cheap labor—very large industrial centers and poor farming communities offering cheap labor, including women and children. In order to exploit the supply of cheap city labor, large snuff, smoking tobacco and cigarette factories are located in Jersey City, New York, Philadelphia and Chicago. Although the raw leaf for cigarettes is grown in North Carolina and Virginia, about fifty per cent of the entire output is made in New York City where machine operators can be engaged cheaply. In the tables on the next page is presented the geographical distribution of manufactures of tobacco and snuff and cigarettes.

In consequence of the importance of machinery and mechanical inventions in the manufacture of cigarettes this industry was the first branch of the trade to display a marked concentration in localization as well as in ownership. Hence it will not surprise us to learn that the American Tobacco Company began its activities in the direction of combination in the manufacture of cigarettes where a combination seemed feasible and practicable.

DISTRIBUTION AND LOCALIZATION OF MANUFACTURES OF TOBACCO AND SNUFF.

State.	1880. %	1885. %	1890. %	1895. %	1900. %	1905. %	Chief products.	Principal manufacturing centers.
Missouri	9	15	27	21	26	20	Plug smoking tobacco.	St. Louis.
North Carolina	8	8	9	9	13	18	Smoking tobacco.	Durham and Winston.
Kentucky	5	8	8	13	12	11	Plug smoking tobacco.	Louisville.
New Jersey	13	11	10	8	7	8	Smoking tobacco, snuff, plug.	Jersey City.
Virginia	26	21	14	12	8	7	Plug smoking tobacco.	Richmond.
Ohio	7	6	9	7	6	7	Plug.	Cincinnati.
Michigan	2	4.5	6	6	2.5	5	Smoking tobacco and plug.	Detroit.
Illinois	7	4	3	4	3.5	3	Smoking tobacco and fine-cut.	Chicago.
Maryland	3.5	3.5	5	3	4	4	Smoking tobacco and snuff.	Baltimore.
Tennessee	.1	.5	.5	.5	1.5	2	Snuff, plug-smoking tobacco.	Nashville.

DISTRIBUTION AND LOCALIZATION OF MANUFACTURES OF CIGARETTES.

State.	1880. %	1885. %	1890. %	1895. %	1900. %	1905. %	Principal manufacturing centers.
New York	72	81	47	52	51	60	New York City.
Virginia	9	...	23	20	22	16	Richmond.
North Carolina	...	5	23	20	19	3	Durham.
Louisiana	...	...	...	...	1	10	New Orleans.

Along with the integration and concentration of production came a more scientifically organized selling market. The extremely high profits enjoyed by the retailer in the sale of cigars is in striking contrast with the rate of profits in the sale of manufactured tobacco. In the former, as we learned above, the rate averaged from 75 to 100 per cent of the selling price; whereas in the latter it approximates 25 per cent. Where the Trust control is strongest and competition least active, profits are lowest, as in cigarettes, in the sale of which gross profits for the retailer are only 20 per cent.

The predominating influence of machinery in the production of plug, chewing tobacco and cigarettes has enabled our manufacturers to compete abroad, which is impossible in the cigar industry because of the relative cheapness of foreign labor. Our exported manufactured tobacco products, in 1905, of $5,000,000 are practically restricted to plug, chewing tobacco and cigarettes. A detailed study of our foreign trade will be attempted in a later chapter. We refer to our foreign trade here merely as an illustration of the close relation between the particular character of the organization of an industry, with respect to capital and labor, and the marketing of goods in general.

In this chapter it has been our aim to interpret the development of the manufacture of tobacco in the light of technical improvements and of changes in the character of the selling market: the former working internally and the latter externally to transform the organization of the industry. The dependence of a cigar industry upon skilled labor and little fixed capital gave rise to a domestic system of production, which in turn resulted in the organization of a selling market along local and personal lines. Large-scale production, which originally resulted from economies in the purchasing of raw material, is moving rapidly toward further concentration under the stimulus of machine production. The giant factory of one thousand workers has not yet succeeded, however, in dislodging completely the small shop employing no more than five men. The vast number of the latter, as many as 20,000 scattered throughout the country, still produce about 25 per cent of the entire output, and employ an even larger proportion of the entire number of workers. In the manufacturing of all other forms of tobacco, machinery and fixed capital have been more important than labor and hence the small producer has been entirely crowded out of the market. The economy of large scale production led to concentration of ownership, which finally culminated in the Tobacco Trust.

The conditions of production in the cigar industry made possible a labor organization which has been able to protect the interests of the worker. In the other branches of the industry, however, where only unskilled labor is required, the position of the worker must necessarily be different.

We have purposely avoided a thorough discussion of these last two problems—the Trust movement and the labor problem—since both are reserved for more extended study in the two succeeding chapters.

APPENDIX

COMPARATIVE SUMMARY OF MANUFACTURES OF TOBACCO SHOWING CAPITAL INVESTMENT, NUMBER OF WAGE-EARNERS AND VALUE OF PRODUCT

FOR ALL PRODUCTS COMBINED—PLUG, CHEWING TOBACCO, SNUFF, SMOKING TOBACCO, CIGARS, CIGARETTES, ETC.

	1880.	1890.	1900.	1905.
Capital[1]	$38,905,950	$90,359,234	$111,527,318	$324,082,501
Wage-earners	86,053	116,790	142,526	159,408
Value of product[2]	125,773,631	195,563,862	263,713,173	330,117,681

The above table is based on *Census of Manufactures, 1905, United States.*

[1] Capital excludes stocks, etc., of corporation. It represents assets of the factory in operation.

[2] Product is valued at the factory and corresponds to cost of production.

CHAPTER IV

THE TOBACCO TRUST

UNLIKE many of our large industrial combinations, the Tobacco Trust does not owe its success to discriminatory transportation rates or monopolistic control of the supply of raw material, which have been predominating influences in the development of the Standard Oil Company, the United States Steel Corporation and other large trusts. Neither can its achievements be attributed primarily to the monopolistic possession of any superior method of production protected by patent rights. Similarly with respect to the marketing and sale of goods, it has enjoyed no resources denied, legally or politically, to its competitors. In a word, the Tobacco Trust stands forth as a conspicuous example of that type of industrial combination which owes merely to the magnitude of its working capital those advantages in production and distribution which enable it to crush competitors until it is in possession of a large part of the entire market. To discover what these specific advantages are and how they have been utilized in overcoming competition, is the main burden of this chapter. We have singled out for extended analysis only those features of the Trust which serve to characterize and explain its development. These are conveniently presented under the following heads: (1) genesis and history; (2) methods of competition; (3) economic advantages; (4) monopolistic features; (5) legal aspect; (6) financial operations and organization.

The genesis of the trust. Up to the middle of the nineties, cigar production, as we learned in the preceding chapter, was—as it is still to some extent—carried on under the household or domestic system. Machinery had not yet found its way into the industry. As a consequence, production as well as distribution, lay in many hands. The small producer, with his shop of three employees and a working capital of $1500, supplied the local retailer in his particular neighborhood. In 1890 there were no less than 23,000 of these small producers, with an average annual output of $5000. An industry so decentralized was not prepared for any large concentration of interests, much less was it susceptible to a trust form of organization.

In the manufacture and sale of plug, chewing tobacco, smoking tobacco, and snuff, conditions were more favorable for an amalgamation of interests. Improved machine production and modern methods of marketing goods led gradually to the extinction of the petty and local manufacturer and to the rise of large producers, catering to an extensive world market. In 1890 an output valued at $65,000,000 was produced in only 395 establishments, employing on the average from fifty to one thousand workers. The smaller factories had each an annual output of $100,000. Some leading brands, like "Duke's Mixture" and "Seal Skin," had a demand extending over several states. Notwithstanding this, there was no sign of a combination of interests in this branch of the industry until the American Tobacco Company began in the middle of the nineties to absorb and annex it to its successfully centralized cigarette business.

It was in the cigarette industry that the germ of the modern trust was planted. From the outset cigarettes were a machine product, and the business always lay in few hands.[1] Subsequent to the introduction of several efficient machines, about 1890, principally the "Bonsack" and the "Eliot," came a war of destructive competition among the large producers in their struggle for the market. During this wasteful contest it occurred to Mr. J. B. Duke, the owner of the "Bonsack" machine, to attempt an organization of the largest manufacturers. At that time (1890) ninety-five per cent of the entire output was produced in four cities; New York City, Rochester, (N. Y.), Durham and Richmond. The five constituent companies[2] that formed the original American Tobacco Company controlled probably eighty-five per cent of the cigarette trade.[3] Combination in the cigarette industry was furthermore relatively easier since the entire output was valued at $9,000,000 compared with $60,000,000 for manufactured tobacco, and $100,000,000 for cigars.[4] In explaining the origin of the Tobacco Trust in the cigarette industry, the above three factors must be considered together:

(1) Technical conditions of production, requiring a large capital investment, and making for large-scale production and concentration;

(2) Invention of machinery, leading to keen and wasteful competition to escape from which a combination of interests was a natural remedy;

[1] *Cf.* pp. 97, 98.

[2] W. Duke and Sons (N. Y. City and Durham), Allen and Ginter (Richmond), W. S. Kimball (Rochester, N. Y.), Goodwin and Co. (N. Y. City), Kinney Tob. Co. (N. Y. City and Richmond).

[3] Mr. Duke estimated the original control at 80 to 90 per cent. *Cf.* N. Y. State Legislative *Investigation of Trusts*, 1897, p. 865.

[4] The entire output of cigarettes (annually) was 2,230,000,000; estimating it at $4.00 per M. (which was high in 1890), the entire value would approximate $9,000,000.

(3) The size and extent of the industry offered no serious obstacle.

The five constituent[1] cigarette companies were organized, in 1890, into a single corporation, The American Tobacco Company, with a capital stock of $25,000,000. There were now under a single control the largest cigarette factories, favorably located, equipped with the most efficient machinery, possessing the leading brands, and having about 85 per cent of the entire output of the country. Still it exercised then no monopolistic control. When the Eliot machine was released by the courts from the injunction imposed upon it, independent manufacturers were able to produce and compete on equal terms with the American Tobacco Company. Since it was impossible to control the supply of raw material, as its cultivation could easily be extended, direct competition in the selling market was the only weapon open to the Trust in its efforts to control the market. As far as we are able to learn, railroad rate discrimination was not enjoyed by the Trust in its contest with adversaries. Besides, transportation charges constitute so small a part of the total cost of production that it could not have been a decisive factor, even if it were practiced.

It was by a long-drawn battle of cut-throat competition that independent producers were forced to surrender. The most dangerous foe of the Trust was the National Cigarette and Tobacco Company, which was able to retail a package of "Admiral" cigarettes (twenty) for five cents, in direct competition with the famous Trust brand "Sweet Caporal," retailing ten for five cents. The Trust immediately began to offer to jobbers its leading and popular brands at cost price. The National Cigarette and Tobacco Com-

[1] *Supra*, p. 103, footnote 2.

pany could not hold out very long against the Trust with its immense capital. One by one the independent producers felt the deadly effect of competitive methods which we shall presently describe in detail. As early as 1896 the American Tobacco Company was practically in control of the greatest part of the entire cigarette market. The largest independent companies were finally absorbed, among which were the National Tobacco Works of Louisville, the T. H. Hall Cigarette Company of New York, and the Consolidated Cigarette Company, New York. In 1897 the American Tobacco Company was one of the several Trusts investigated by a committee of the New York State Legislature, as a result of which the directors were later indicted.[1]

But legislative investigations and legal indictments did not check the growth of the Trust. By 1898 its capital stock had increased to $70,000,000, much of which had been invested in the manufacture and sale of other products—plug, chewing tobacco, smoking tobacco and snuff.

This brings us to the second stage in the development of the Tobacco Trust—the concentration of the tobacco manufactures.[2] This step seemed as inevitable as it was feasible. In the first place, most of the large cigarette factories that were absorbed by the American Tobacco Company also produced, to some extent, these other products—plug and smoking tobacco, etc. Furthermore, it was apparent that the control of the sale of cigarettes to retailers was an entering wedge for the control of other products. By offering special rebates

[1] *Investigation of Trusts*, by New York State Legislature, 1897.

[2] Used here in the technical sense—manufactures of plug, smoking tobacco, chewing tobacco and snuff.

on leading cigarette brands, the Trust induced the retailer to push its new brands of plug and smoking tobacco. In 1891 the American Tobacco Company purchased three large producers of manufactured tobacco—the National Tobacco Works, Marburg Bros,, and Gail and Ax Company. In 1895 it absorbed the very large firms of James G. Butler Tobacco Works (St. Louis) and the P. Lorilard Company of New Jersey. Many less important manufacturers also came into the Trust fold.[1]

After purchasing the large plug interests of The Drummond Tobacco Company and the Brown Tobacco Company of St. Louis, the movement culminated in October, 1898, in the organization of the "Continental Tobacco Company," with a capital stock of $75,000,000. This was confessedly a creature of the American Tobacco Company, having for its avowed purpose the concentration and control of the plug interests of the country. The capital which the American Tobacco Company had invested in the manufacture of plug was transferred to the Continental Company in exchange for $30,000,000 of common stock of this new company. Mr. J. B. Duke was president of both companies—The American Tobacco Company and the Continental Tobacco Company. In its official announcement the Continental stated that it owned "the properties, rights, trade-marks, names, and assets, etc.," of the following concerns: John Finzer & Bros., Louisville, Ky.; P. H. Mayo & Co., Richmond, Va.; Daniel Scotty & Co., Detroit, Mich.; P. T. Sorg Co., Middletown, O.; Drummond Tobacco Co., St. Louis, Mo.; J. Wright Co., Richmond, Va.; Wright

[1] Among others were P. Whitlock Co., Richmond; Heinshein & Co., New Orleans; Ellis & Co., Baltimore; A. H. Motley & Co., Reldsville, N. C. *Cf. N. Y. State Legislative Investigation of Trusts*, 1897, p. 863.

Bros. Tobacco Co., St. Charles, Mo.; P. Lorillard Company, New Jersey ($3,000,000 stock); American Tobacco Company's plug interests. The largest single plug producers, Liggett and Myers, of St. Louis, controlling no less than fifteen per cent of the entire trade, refused to amalgamate with the Trust, except upon terms more favorable to itself than the Trust offered. The Trust began immediately to encroach upon the markets of this firm, by selling the finished product ten per cent below the standard price, besides offering premiums to salesmen.[1] Liggett and Myers retaliated with a similar cut in prices. This competitive war was carried on for several months, when the Trust finally bought out its competitor (April, 1899) at a figure that seems abnormally inflated. The Trust paid $12,500,000 for the entire plant, which was equivalent to $1366 for each $100 share of stock of the absorbed company.[2] To raise the sum necessary for this purchase, as well as to facilitate the absorption of two more companies,[3] the Continental issued $25,000,000 new stock. The stock issued seems often to have been out of proportion to the value of the properties absorbed by the Trust.

According to the first annual report of the Continental Tobacco Company, its capital stock was $100,000,000, and its combined output of plug annually was 130,000,000 pounds.[4] This implied that seventy-five per cent of the entire plug production was now in control of the Tobacco Trust, which, for several years past, also controlled a similar proportion of the cigarette trade. The

[1] *Cf. Commercial and Financial Chronicle*, vol. 67, p. 841 (1898).

[2] *Ibid.*, Oct. 2, 1898.

[3] The Union Tobacco Co., of Albany, and The Buchanan and Lyall Co., Brooklyn.

[4] *Cf. Commercial and Financial Chronicle*, vol. 70 (1900), p. 738.

Continental was launched with the aid of the Standard Oil influence. Messrs. O. H. Payne and Thomas F. Ryan remained actively interested in the future promotions of the Tobacco Trust, the latter being a director until his resignation in 1906.

In 1901 the two companies—the American Tobacco Company and the Continental—were amalgamated into a holding company of New Jersey, known as the Consolidated Tobacco Company. Although the avowed purpose of this new organization was to harmonize the interests of the two companies, it so happened that in the process of amalgamation the insiders incidentally pocketed a large part of the surplus funds, by methods which have long since come to be associated with "high finance."

The operations of the Trust did not cease with the control of the markets for cigarettes, plug, smoking tobacco and chewing tobacco. In March, 1900, came a consolidation of the snuff business through the launching of a new concern, the American Snuff Company, with a capital stock of $23,000,000. As in the formation of the plug Trust, so here, the nucleus was the property and the factories of the American Tobacco Company. The latter sold its interests for $4,500,000 to the American Snuff Company, which was from the first a subsidiary organ of the Trust. The first official statement of the American Snuff Company showed that it owned in fee simple, or held the majority stock of the following snuff concerns: Atlantic Snuff Company, Philadelphia, Pa.; George W. Helme Co., Helmetta, N. J.; Southern Snuff Company, Memphis, Tenn.; Bruton & Condon, Nashville, Tenn.; Steward Snuff Company, Clarksville, Tenn.; W. E. Geret & Sons, Philadelphia, Pa.; Steward Ralph Snuff Company, Philadelphia, Pa.; Dental Snuff Company, Lynchburg, Va.; Helmetta Mercantile Co,, Helmetta. N.

J.; Bowers Snuff Co. (American Tob. Co. Plant), Changewater, N. J.; P. Lorillard Company's plant at Jersey City. Their total output in 1900 approximated fifteen million pounds, which was practically the entire snuff production of the country. The total output to-day is twenty-two million pounds, of which the Trust controls probably ninety per cent.

In 1901 began the Trust movement for the assimilation of the cigar industry. In that year was organized the American Cigar Company, with a capital stock of $10,000,000 with which to buy up independent manufacturers. An auspicious beginning was made in the purchase of one of the largest and best known producers of domestic cigars,—Smith, Powell and Company. This was followed in the same year by the absorption of the Hummel-Vogt Company of Louisville, and the P. Whitlock Cheroot Factory of Richmond, Va. Shortly afterwards the independents were startled by the report, which later proved to be authentic, announcing the purchase by the Trust of two very large independent producers,—the Brown Brothers Company of Detroit, having a capacity of 40,000,000 cigars annually, and the Roth, Bruner & Feist Company of Cincinnati. To keep pace with, as well as to hasten, the process of absorption, the capital stock of the American Cigar Company had been increased from $10,000,000 in 1901 to $40,000,000 in 1906. Negotiations are now pending (March, 1907) for the absorption by the Trust of the largest independent concern manufacturing domestic cigars, namely, the United Cigar Manufacturers Company, having a capital stock of $20,000,000, and controlling seven per cent of the entire output of the country.[1]

[1] The United Cigar Manufacturers Company comprises the three larg-

It is difficult to ascertain what proportion of the domestic cigar industry is now in the hands of the Trust; but it probably does not exceed twenty-five per cent. Several reasons may be assigned for the slow headway made by the Trust in this branch of the industry. As we pointed out in the preceding chapter, the cigar industry has been organized on a petty basis, on the side of production as well as of distribution. We learned, in that connection, how, until the introduction of bunch-making machines, the Trust had no decisive advantages over the small producer. Even to-day, the large independent manufacturer can produce cigars as cheaply as the Trust. To secure a monopoly of further inventions of cigar machinery, the Trust bought control of the International Machine Company, which held patent-rights on some recent inventions.[1]

Turning to distribution, the Trust discovered that the selling market was not susceptible to easy control. In the sale of manufactured tobacco, a single retailer usually markets all products; so that once the Trust has secured a foothold with the retailer in any particular product, say cigarettes, it is relatively simpler to extend control over the sale of the other commodities—plug, chewing and smoking tobacco and snuff—than it is to gain control over many retailers who carry in stock only cigars. In the latter case the undertaking is equivalent to gaining control over a new industry. The Trust is further handi-

est single establishments in the country—Kerbs, Wertheim and Schiffer; Hirshorn, Mack and Co.; Straiton & Storm Company. Their net earnings in 1905 were $1,262,787.

[1] It was reported recently in the *Tobacco Trade Journal*, Feb. 19, 1907, that the Trust had installed in its factories at Kingston, N. Y., some new cigar machines which perform automatically all the processes from making of the bunch to wrapping the cigar and cutting off the "tuck."

capped by the fact that its goods are non-union. The Union label is an important factor in the retail cigar trade. Over twenty per cent of the entire output bears the label.

With no decisive advantages in production over the large independent producers and with the retail market organized on a petty, local, and personal basis, the Trust found it necessary to invent new instruments with which it could overcome some of the initial obstacles in its path. It decided upon the organization of its own retail agencies as the most effective means of capturing the cigar market. Here was a direct method of placing the Trust goods in the hands of the consumer without the aid of a middleman, either wholesaler or retailer. The chain system of the United Cigar stores has been remarkably successful. The Trust has to-day something like one thousand stores, located in every large city in the United States. It is said to have over three hundred in New York City. Every advance in the control of the retail market means an added step in the direction of concentration in production. A further extension of the chain system of retail agencies is the recent organization of the National Cigar Stands Company, which aims to control the cigar trade of drug stores. This subsidiary company of the Trust already controls the retail cigar stands in the leading drug stores of the country. The National Cigar Stands Company supplies the outfit, show-case, all advertisements, and window display, on condition that the proprietor of the drug store, besides paying a small rental fee for the use of the outfit, consent to carry only such goods as are permitted by the National Cigar Stands Company. Although the United Cigar Store Company has declared a seven per cent dividend annually for three years, the American Cigar Company, through which the Trust conducts its cigar manufacturing business, has not yet declared any dividends on its common stock.[1] The Trust controls the stogie trade through the American Stogie Company, which produces practically the entire output of the country. It has a capital stock of $12,000,000.

The most profitable branch of the cigar industry is the manufacture and sale of Havana goods, domestic and Cuban made. In 1902 the Trust began operations to absorb this trade. The Cuban manufacturers were already largely concentrated in three companies, the Henry Clay and Bock Company (an English concern), The Havana Commercial Company (an American Company), and the Cubanas Company. In 1902 the Consolidated Tobacco Company, which was then the Trust holding Company, secured control of each of these three companies, which were ultimately (1902) merged into the present Havana Tobacco Company.[2] Although the Trust controls about fifty per cent of the Cuban-made cigar trade, the Havana Tobacco Company has never succeeded in earning dividends for its common stock, which has generally been quoted below thirty on the market and in 1906 went down to ten. It is said that the reputation which the Cuban cigar once possessed in America and in Germany is now being impaired under the Trust control, as a result of a deterioration both in the quality of leaf and in the workmanship employed in its manufacture. The largest American importers of Havana goods are Park and Tilford, and the Waldorf Segar Company, both handling, almost exclusively, goods of independent (non-Trust) manufacturers.

[1] It has outstanding to-day $20,000,000 four per cent gold bonds, $10,000,000 six per cent preferred, $10,000,000 common stock.

[2] *Cf. Commercial and Financial Chronicle*, vol. 74, p. 1142 (1902).

An interesting chapter in the development of the Trust is its movement in foreign markets that were open to competition.[1] The American Tobacco Company was so successful in Japan that the government was forced to take over the industry; the profits which seemed on the verge of passing into the coffers of the Trust, now go to the government treasury.[2] In 1901 the Trust caused consternation among the German manufacturers by obtaining control of the Jasmatzi cigarette works of Dresden, and purchasing later some minor concerns. The outcome of the struggle for the German market is still undecided. In 1902 the Mexican tobacco interests passed into the hands of the Trust at a cost of $9,000,000.

The most interesting phase, however, of the Trust movement abroad came in Great Britain. The story is a long one and filled with many exciting incidents, of which, here, only the important can be mentioned. In 1901 the Ogdens Limited, a large company of Liverpool, was bought up by the British Tobacco Company, a creature of the American Trust. The Ogdens Company immediately began to cut prices on cigarettes to English jobbers. This led the independent manufacturers and wholesalers to combine their interests, and they organized the Imperial Tobacco Company[3] to fight the American Trust. The competitive struggle between the two

[1] The governments of France, Italy, Austria, Spain and some minor European countries exercise a moncpoly (Régie) over the tobacco trade.

[2] Japan's complete monopoly of tobacco went into effect in 1904. It now not only exercises control over the sale of leaf as formerly (1896–1904), but also directs the sale of the manufactured product, from which it derives a large revenue.

[3] The Imperial Tobacco Company was comprised of the thirteen largest manufacturers of Great Britain, and had a capital stock of one hundred million dollars.

giant companies was intense and wasteful to both parties. The Imperial offered to distribute annually $750,000 to those dealers who agreed not to handle, for a period of years, goods of the American Company. Ogdens Limited retaliated by offering to dealers who agreed to handle their goods (not exlusively) for four years, a participation in the net profits of the Ogdens Company besides a bonus of $1,000,000 annually. About 4,500 English dealers were induced to accept the enticing offer of the Ogdens Limited, in which it promised to distribute pro rata annually, $1,200,000 ($1,000,000 bonus and $200,000 net profits.) Such a procedure meant a losing game for the American and the English manufacturers, and consequently something had to be done to remedy the situation. The natural outcome resulted: the two companies came to an understanding. The Imperial Company paid Mr. Duke, head of the American Trust, $7,500,000, as a bonus for withdrawing from the markets of Great Britain. The American interests, moreover, were given an option on one-third of the $100,000,000 stock of the Imperial Company. To prevent a repetition of wasteful competition in neutral foreign markets, the British-American Tobacco Company was organized to control the trade. The Imperial (English) Company was given a one-third share of the $30,000,000 stock of the British-American Company, the American interests reserving two-thirds. The former has six and the latter twelve representatives on the board of directors, of which Mr. Duke is President.

But what about the agreement which the Ogdens Limited had made with the 4500 English tobacco dealers? The latter claimed that when the Imperial purchased the Ogdens Company, it assumed legal responsibility for *all* its contracts, including the one which entailed a distribution of about $11,500,000 to the dealers in return for their agreement to handle the goods of the Ogdens Limited.[1] The case was carried into court, finally reached the Court of Appeals, which decided in favor of the British dealers, and against Mr. Duke and the Imperial Company. A settlement was finally made, favorable to the dealers.[2] The important point to remember is that the American Trust displayed its real fighting force as a competitor in the English market and that it brought about an understanding between the largest English and American producers.

In 1904 a reorganization of the Trust occurred, whereby the three companies—the original American Tobacco Company, the Continental Tobacco Company, and the Consolidated Tobacco Company (a holding company) were merged into one. By this merger all the property, plants, capital stock, etc., of the parent and subsidiary companies passed into the control of a single corporation—the American Tobacco Company of New Jersey, with an authorized capital of $300,000,000, but with an actual issue of $251,710,000. Besides controlling about seventy-five per cent of the entire American trade in cigarettes, plug, chewing and smoking tobacco, and snuff, and about twenty-five per cent of the cigar indus-

[1] The dealers were promised an annual bonus, for four years, of $1,000,000. But they also demanded their share of the $7,500,000, which Mr. Duke received as bonus for withdrawing from the field, claiming that this was part of the profits of the Ogdens Limited, which profits were, by contract, to be distributed to them. Mr. Duke, on the other hand, maintained that, when he received the bonus from the Imperial he was acting in his personal, not official, capacity, and consequently the bonus was not part of the profits of the Ogdens Limited.

[2] For detailed information concerning the Trust movement in England, *cf. Commercial and Financial Chronicle*, vol. 74, p. 632; vol. 75, p. 735.

try, it also possesses its own licorice plant, tin-foil factory, pipe manufacturing company, machine company and retail as well as wholesale agencies and controls directly some tobacco land in Cuba and in the United States. Since 1904, its activities have expanded. The real magnitude of this $450,000,000 Trust will be more fully appreciated when we consider, in another connection, its financial operations. The circle of the Trust organization is now practically complete from the ownership or control of tobacco lands to the manufacture of products and the marketing of goods. In no other industry has there been developed so complete and so splendid an organization as the Tobacco Trust.

So much for its genesis and history. The question which naturally suggests itself is, how did it attain its present power? As we stated at the outset, its development has not depended upon any railroad-rate discrimination or legal franchise denied to its competitors, nor upon the ownership of the supply of raw material. Nor has its success been the result of any advantages or economies in production such as are usually claimed for the trust form of organization. In our opinion very little economy in production is achieved by extending the size of a tobacco establishment beyond the point already attained by large independent manufacturers. Such economies as the Tobacco Trust has enjoyed, may or may not redound ultimately to its advantage. That its present position has been due to these economies, cannot be maintained. It is our belief that its supremacy has been gained by, and still rests upon, the employment of methods of competition which are ordinarily considered unfair; and that these methods are made possible and practicable by the mere size of its working capital. It is to a detailed consideration of some of these methods of competition that we will now direct our attention.

Methods of Competition. The most familiar as well as the most effective method has been that of "local competition"—underselling a single competitor in his own limited market, while sustaining prices elsewhere. This device is feasible only for large companies that can make temporary sacrifices for the possibility of greater returns in the future. Its efficiency has been so often demonstrated, particularly by the Standard Oil Company, that we need not multiply instances in the case of the Tobacco Trust. In the early nineties to check the sale of "Admiral" cigarettes manufactured by an independent concern (The National Cigarette Company), the American Tobacco Company offered its leading brand, "Sweet Caporal" cigarettes, at cost price *exclusively* in regions where the Admiral was being successfully marketed. The National Company surrendered soon afterward. In 1901, the American Tobacco Company was selling "American Beauty" cigarettes for $1.50 per thousand, less two per cent discount for cash, when the Revenue Tax alone was $1.50 per thousand. This was done, however, *only* where the Wells-Whitehead Company had succeeded in marketing its most popular brand, the "North Carolina Bright" cigarette.[1] New York jobbers found that by purchasing their cigarettes from North Carolina jobbers, after paying a slight premium in addition to freight charges, they would pay less for them than by buying direct from the Trust in New York City. Again, in 1906 the Ware-Kramer Tobacco Company of Norfolk, Va., entered a complaint with the Bureau of Corporations, charging the Trust "with maintaining one price on their products in the North and another in South." In the North the Trust price for cigarettes was from $3.90 to $4.00 per

[1] *Cf. Report of Industrial Commission*, vol. 13, pp. 337-338.

thousand, whereas in the South, where the Ware-Kramer Company was marketing its goods, the price on the same brand was reduced to $3.15 and $3.25 per thousand.

This local competition which helped to build up the Cigarette Trust, was practiced in the sale of other products. During the struggle for the plug market between the Continental and the large independent producers, Liggett and Myers, the former was offering its "Battle Ax" brand for thirteen cents per pound, which was below the cost of production since the tax was six cents and the raw leaf seven cents per pound. After Liggett and Myers was absorbed, "Battle Ax" rose to thirty cents per pound.[1] To what extent local competition can be carried on may be judged from the success achieved by the Trust in England and Japan.

An instrument frequently employed in making this local competition effective, is that known as the "Factors' Agreement," or the "Consignment Agreement," whereby the jobber is offered special rebates for agreeing to handle Trust goods exclusively, or to boycott independent brands. While a two and one-half per cent commission was allowed jobbers who did not discriminate against Trust goods; seven and one-half per cent was given to those who handled Trust goods exclusively.

There is published in the "Investigation of Trusts"[2] a long list of jobbers whose orders for Trust goods were not filled because they carried in stock independent goods. To injure the marketing of goods manufactured by the United States Tobacco Company, the Trust altered its price list whereby the jobber was to receive

[1] *Cf. Report of Industrial Commission*, p. 339.

[2] *Cf. Investigation of Trusts* by N. Y. State Legislature, 1897, pp. 913-921; also *Report of Ind. Com.*, vol. 13, pp. 333-335.

not as formerly, a uniform profit of two cents per pound, but one cent profit outright, and a five and one-half per cent special discount, provided he handled only Trust goods.[1] Although Mr. Duke in his testimony before the Industrial Commission in 1901 stated that the Trust no longer employed this Factors' Agreement, it was shown in court only recently (1906) that it was still in vogue in Massachusetts, since it was proved conclusively that special rebates were given to jobbers who agreed not to handle certain independent brands.[2] The large jobbing concern of E. Locker Company of Brooklyn, was recently unable to have its orders filled by the Trust, the Courts holding that the Trust had the legal right to refuse to sell to whomsoever it saw fit.[3] This Factors' Agreement is especially potent in crushing any new competition in markets already controlled by the Trust, for the jobber is loath to risk his assured profits, derived from the sale of established Trust brands, in exchange for the doubtful income from new, independent goods. Under such conditions potential as well as actual competition is reduced to a minimum. In a recent speech, Mr. H. D. Mills, President of the Independent Tobacco Manufacturers Association, said, "that the Trust had the jobbers, who are the distributing agencies of manufactured goods, in such a position that it was almost impossible in some sections of the country for independent manufacturers,

[1] *Report of Industrial Commission*, vol. 13, p. 306.

[2] *Cf.* Case of Commonwealth (Mass.) *vs.* Strauss, 1906. While the Trust won its case on some technicality, the courts upheld the constitutionality of the State Law forbidding this practice.

[3] The Trust was interested in building up its own wholesale agency in Greater New York, and hence refused to supply independent jobbers with their established brands. The Metropolitan Tob. Co., a Trust concern, is now in control of the N. Y. jobbing market. *Cf.* E. Locker & Co. *vs.* The American Tobacco Co. (N. Y., 1906).

even though they had an established trade on their goods (elsewhere), to get them distributed;" that is, in territories controlled by the Trust.[1]

Closely allied to the methods of local competition and the Factors' Agreement, is that known as "Brand Imitation." This is a most direct form of destructive competition: it consists in selling at reduced prices brands which are apparently imitations of popular brands of independent manufacturers. A recent instance of this is the marketing at a low figure by the Trust of the "Central Union" smoking tobacco in direct competition with the "Union Leader" of the United States Tobacco Company.[2] The Trust distributed its "Central Union" free of charge to jobbers, in order to ruin the "Union Leader." It was not until the reputation of the independent brand had been seriously damaged, that the courts enjoined the Trust from further free distribution, where the intent to injure the property of another was so apparent. Similarly the Trust marketed at a low price a brand in imitation of the "Qboid" tobacco manufactured by Larus and Brothers, Richmond, Va. The Trust is also charged with having purchased large quantities of popular brands and having offered them to the public at a ridiculously low price in order to bias the public against its real merit and quality, the assumption being that a brand, a cigar, for instance, that sells below price, say two for five cents, must be of an inferior grade. As the value of a brand is one of the important assets in the tobacco trade, these methods are very ruinous to independent manufacturers who cannot withstand a persistent attack from the Trust.

[1] *Cf. Tobacco*, trade journal (weekly), N. Y., Oct. 25, 1905.

[2] *Cf.* U. S. Tobacco Co. *vs*. The American Tobacco Co., and McGreeny and Maning, 1925 Mass.

Another means of underselling competitors is the use of the *coupon system*, whereby the consumer receives a premium certificate equivalent to a ten per cent rebate. The coupon system is especially valuable in the tobacco trade because it serves as a substitute for the cutting of prices; the latter being difficult, owing to the existence of conventional and convenient prices, five cents and multiples of five. It is more feasible to give coupons than to reduce a five-cent cigar to four cents. Since much of the tobacco trade is transient, the successful operation of the "premium" plan depends upon a wide distribution of stores that offer the coupons, as through a chain of retail agencies like the United Cigar Stores. Recognizing the impracticality of this system for individual producers catering to a limited market, the independent manufacturers have adopted a general stamp or trade-mark for all independent brands.[1]

We have already spoken of the operation of the Trust retail stores as an added source of direct income through the elimination of the middleman's profits. Equally important are the incidental advantages derived from this organization of the retail agencies. It is often employed as a weapon in driving out of business those retailers who incur the disfavor of the Trust. The installation of a United Cigar Store is a signal for the independent retailer to beat a retreat. Nor must we overlook its value as an advertising medium for Trust brands. When the consumer has been educated by the United Cigar Stores to the use of Trust goods he is likely to continue his demand for them in independent as well as Trust stores.

The Tobacco Trust has developed a unique method of

[1] The leading independent manufacturers are in this association. *Cf. Tobacco* (trade journal), N. Y., Oct. 28, 1905.

competition in its efforts to curtail the sale of any particular line of goods which it desires to keep off the market.[1] In order to check the growing popularity of "scrap" goods, the Trust has made its sale unprofitable for manufacturers by increasing the price of raw material. To compete with plug and chewing tobacco, the scrap leaf must be bought for no higher than ten cents, which was the maximum price for a number of years. When the Trust decided, however, that scrap goods must not come into competition with their products, it forced up the market for scrap-cuttings until its price reached twenty-five cents per pound. This necessitated an increase in the selling price to retailers, who found it unprofitable to market their goods. Where the retailers did continue to carry it in stock, the Trust sold their scrap goods at the old price, which, of course, the independent manufacturers could not do without loss. The result was that some of the large independent manufacturers of scrap goods were driven out of business or absorbed by the Trust.

These have been, and are still, some of the methods employed by the Trust in obtaining control of the market and in crushing all dangerous rivals. Its policy has been to balk at no temporary expenditure for the sake of ultimately capturing the market. Large independent manufacturers maintain that with the selling agencies open to them on fair terms, they can compete successfully with the Trust; the implication being that the latter has no decisive advantageson over its rivals in producti. The present contest may be likened to a struggle between two contending armies, possessing equal skill, and differing only in numerical size; the larger one by tem-

[1] "Scrap" smoking and chewing tobacco was being substituted for plug and standard chewing tobacco, over which products the Trust exercises a large control.

porarily sacrificing greater numbers can ultimately overcome the smaller foe. It seems like the victory of sheer brute force, which in the case of the Tobacco Trust takes the form of the large working capital fund, which enables it: (1) to undersell in local markets for a considerable length of time, while sustaining prices elsewhere; (2) to offer special rebates and discounts to jobbers who discriminate against independent manufacturers; (3) to distribute free, or sell below the market price, imitation brands in order to injure competitors, which it can do for some time even at the risk of incurring damages for legal infringement; (4) to establish a premium coupon system as well as the organization of its own retail agencies, which are employed incidentally to drive out of business those retailers who refuse to obey the Trust orders; (5) and to render business in a certain branch of the industry unprofitable by increasing abnormally the price of raw material. The Trust has at one time or another employed successfully these methods of competition in getting control of the market.

Economic Advantages—There are those, however, who maintain that the Trust owes its position to advantages and economies in production and distribution which accrue only to a Trust form of organization. What these advantages are we now proceed to investigate. In reply to a question concerning these advantages, Mr. J. B. Duke, the President of the Tobacco Trust, stated: "I think the main advantage is in the combination of talent." Though Mr. Duke did not proceed to explain, his idea was probably that the Trust form of organization furnishes the capital necessary for the bringing together of exceptionally able men, as well as supplying the material, so to speak, by which economies can be effected. These economies will be considered from the standpoint, first, of production, and secondly, of distribution.

When the Trust was first organized, in 1890, it had control of the most efficient machine, the *Bonsack*. Shortly afterwards it secured control of the "Allison,"[1] a competing machine. The efficiency of the best organized factory was immediately transferred to all its cigarette plants, and in some cases the less efficient plants were entirely dismantled. The producing capacity, for instance, of the Goodwin & Company (New York) factory was transferred to a more efficient factory, the W. S. Kimball & Company, Rochester, N. Y. Recently the manufacturing capacity of the Kimball company was removed to the Durham factory (N. C.). The Hall Cigarette Company and the Consolidated Cigarette Company, each employing about four hundred hands, were combined into a new and single factory in New York City.[2] This process of concentration has gone on constantly. When the Continental Company was organized in 1898 and acquired control of the plug interests of St. Louis, the output of the six leading factories was turned over to the two largest and most efficient ones, the Liggett & Myers Company and the Drummond Tobacco Co.

Where the Trust is in possession of some superior and patented machinery there is some economy in concentration, but where it enjoys no such monopolistic right, then the Trust merely hastens the introduction of improved methods of production throughout that part of the industry over which it exercises control. Technical efficiency on the side of production becomes the common property of all the large independent competitors in any industry. A proof of this is the fact that there still exist

[1] Mr. Duke organized the Allison Machine Co. in order to control the Allison Machine. *Cf.* N. Y. State *Investigation of Trusts*, pp. 894, 895.

[2] *Ibid.*, pp. 860, 875.

active competitors in the manufacture and sale of plug, chewing and smoking tobacco, who must surely produce as cheaply as the Trust, since otherwise they could not withstand the advantages which the latter enjoys in marketing its goods.

In two ways the Trust enjoys a slight advantage in the employment of labor. First, by its extensive operations the Trust can shift its productive capacity to those factories where labor is cheapest. The independent producer might also ultimately establish his factory in the locality where labor is cheapest, but he cannot do so with the ease and rapidity possible under a Trust organization, which has many factories located throughout the country. For instance, when it was discovered that cheap child and female labor was available in the South, the Trust dismantled some of its northern factories, and transferred their capacity to Clarksville, Tennessee, and Durham and Winston, North Carolina, where some of its other factories are located. When the Trust was in need of cheap labor for making cigars, it located a factory in the heart of the Italian quarter in New York City where cheap, immigrant labor was available.

A greater saving in labor-costs arises from the employment of non-union workers. The Tobacco Workers Union has not been able to cope with the gigantic Trust. In 1895 the former was so disrupted that it found a reorganization necessary, and to-day it is still very weak both in membership and in actual power. When the plug factories of St. Louis were absorbed by the Trust in 1898, wages declined twenty-five per cent in the Drummond factory.[1] The Trust refuses to bargain col-

[1] *Cf. Report of Industrial Commission*, vol. 8, pp. 399-405; testimony of the President of the Tobacco Workers' Union.

lectively with its workers. On the other hand, the independent manufacturer is not in a position to antagonize the Union. To take advantage of the consumers' anti-Trust sentiment, the independent manufacturer generally unionizes his goods in competition with the non-union goods of the Trust. The difference in wages between union and non-union labor is from ten to twenty per cent. It must be remembered however that wages of labor constitute less than ten per cent of the total cost of production.

In the purchase of leaf, the independent manufacturer stands on the same footing with the Trust. Where the latter has forced prices down, the independent manufacturer has profited equally. Some economy is probably effected by the Trust in being able to use its leaf to the best advantage, since the extent of its manufactures makes possible a finer grading and selection of leaf for each product. As independent factories are located side by side with Trust factories, there is no saving in the transportation of leaf to the factories. There is however some economy for the Trust in the elimination of cross-freighting, since it can fill its orders for finished products from many factories instead of from a single one. As transportation charges form, however, only two per cent of the entire value of the finished product, this economy, though appreciable, cannot be very important as a determining factor in competition for the market.[1]

In the marketing of goods, the Trust does effect some important economies. We have already pointed out the value of advertising and popularizing certain brands.

[1] *Cf. Report of Industrial Commission*, vol. 6, pp. 207–321, for discussion of transportation charges in the distribution of tobacco. *Cf.* also *Twelfth Census*, *Manufactures*, special report on "Tobacco," pp. 650, 660.

There is a double saving for the Trust in the cost of advertising: first, because of the large quantity of material and labor required, the cost per unit of advertising is less; second, its advertising is concentrated on fewer brands, not only reducing the cost per unit, but also getting better returns from this form of advertising.[1]

More important, however, is the reduction or elimination of the jobbers' profit in marketing the finished products to the retailer. In proportion as competition among manufacturers is curtailed, the jobbers and retailers must necessarily sell at a lower margin. Once the Trust is in control of seventy-five per cent of the market for any particular kind of merchandise, it can dictate the conditions under which such goods are to be sold. Jobbers sell to-day on a basis of two per cent gross profit. Where the Trust fails to control the retailer indirectly through the jobber, it can fall back on its own retail agencies, as has already been pointed out. It must be remembered, however, that the economy resulting from a reduction of the jobber's and retailer's profit is the result of an effective control of the market, and is not an original factor in determining the initial success of the Trust.

Another source of economy is the power to demand prompt settlement of all outstanding accounts. The petty manufacturer must frequently wait from two to four months for payment, whereas the Trust's merchandise is paid for within thirty days. Closely akin to this is the economy resulting from the employment of fewer commercial agents not merely in the collection of accounts but in the sale of goods. With the concentration

[1] According to the figures given in the annual reports of the American Tobacco Co., the advertising fund has averaged about $500,000 in the last five years.

of the Tobacco manufacturers in 1898, not only was there a reduction in the number of salesmen, but less expensive men were employed. In the sale of certain long established Trust brands, in cigarettes, plug and smoking tobacco, agents are not required; orders for such being sent by mail.

It must be admitted that some of these advantages imply a social economy, a releasing, so to speak, of social energy. To the extent that the Trust makes possible the operation of its business by fewer men, it is a social economy, and deserves to enjoy the profits arising from it. To the extent that a large quantity of goods can be manufactured by the most efficient machinery, the Trust is likewise socially useful. It is a mistake, however, to believe that it is to these economies that the Tobacco Trust owes its position. These are important, but incidental, advantages which have been made possible only after the Trust has attained success. This success, however, is attributable to the methods of competition, which have already been described.

Monopoly features—In the light of what has been said, are we justified in calling the Tobacco Trust a monopoly? If by this is implied the complete absence of competition, then we are not justified, for in every branch of the tobacco industry, from the purchase of leaf to the sale of the manufactured product, there is at least some competition.[1] But although it has not completely annihilated competition, it has succeeded in preventing it from rising above a certain point.

[1] There is at least one exception; in the manufacture and sale of licorice, it was shown that the Trust did exercise a virtual monopoly. *Cf.* N. Y. State *vs.* MacAndrews, Forbes & Co., 1906. This Trust concern was found guilty of being a conspiracy in restraint of trade. Since this conviction, the price of licorice has fallen considerably.

So long as leaf tobacco can be grown and purchased freely, as is the case; and so long as in the manufacture of tobacco the Trust enjoys no monopolistic privileges entailing the use of superior methods of production; through the possession of patents, etc., and so long as the selling market is organized as at present, preventing absolute control by the Trust; under such conditions there must always be some degree of actual and potential competition. The competitor, however, cannot extend his activity very far without coming into deadly conflict with a foe that is equipped with greater engines of war; for mere size, as shown above, enables the Trust to employ methods of competition denied to any ordinary single competitor. Equal competition can exist now only for an adversary that is armed with as great a capital fund as the Tobacco Trust, and is equally willing and able to make present sacrifices for the sake of larger rewards in the future.

This power of the Trust has been used in two ways: to depress the price of leaf, and to curtail the profits of the middlemen. The fact that the consumer may not suffer from this does not make the Trust less of a monopoly. This monopoly power may consist, not only in reducing the profits of the farmer and jobber, but also in reserving for itself a certain area of industrial activities. It is as if the Trust had put a fence around a section of the industry and warned off competitors with a "no trespassing allowed" sign. In most discussions of the problem this latter function of the Trust is too frequently lost sight of. For the ability to retain and enjoy the ordinary profits of a business which under other, freer conditions, might be lost to competitors is equivalent to a monopoly power. Whether we call it a monopoly or not, that power exists and operates.

Legal aspect—The courts, however, have for the most part not entertained this view. In the case of E. Locker & Company *vs.* the American Tobacco Company, a State Supreme Court held that the mere size of a business, however large, does not make it a monopoly, though it was shown, in this instance, that the Trust controlled eighty per cent of the business. The attorney for the Trust contended that it may be necessary and proper in the course of business "to kill a competitor financially," as was proven to have been done in this case. The plaintiff tried to collect damages from the Trust for the latter's refusal to supply the former with goods. To the plaintiff Judge Marean replied: "you start with the proposition that nine-tenths of the tobacco in the United States is owned by one concern—the American Tobacco Company. It appears to me that you are suffering from the lawful powers that go with such an ownership. I do not understand that they can be compelled to sell you." In New Jersey the courts held that the Tobacco Trust had the legal right to impose upon the jobber as a condition of sale that the latter should not traffic the goods of independent jobbers. While in Massachusetts the Trust is restrained from this practice, it is permitted by law to make "exclusive" sales to jobbers who carry only its goods. In effect there is no practical difference.[1] In Missouri the merger of the tobacco companies was declared to be within the law.[2] In a word, our State courts legalize the methods of competition which have enabled the Trust to attain its present position and control of about seventy-five per cent of the tobacco trade. Under our present system of

[1] Commonwealth *vs.* Strauss, Supreme Court of Mass., (*1906*).

[2] State *vs.* Continental Tobacco Company, 1903.

State laws there is little hope therefore of securing satisfactory regulation of Trusts.

Federal regulation through the operation of the inter-state commerce act is equally ineffectual, since the Supreme Court of the United States declared that *manufacturing* is not in itself inter-state commerce.[1] A compulsory Federal licensing act, like that recommended by President Roosevelt and the recent Commissioner of Corporations, J. A. Garfield, might provide some remedy for existing evils.[2] Should the courts reverse their decisions and declare *manufacturing* to be an act of inter-state commerce, even then this proposed law might be nullified by an arrangement on the part of the Trust whereby its selling and marketing of goods would be confined within state boundaries. So long as there exists this distinction between State and inter-state commerce, the spirit of remedial legislation is apt to be defeated. Plainly what is needed is a thorough-going Federal code regulating commerce and industry, such as Germany enjoys to-day. With respect to some of our largest enterprises the artificial distinction between state and inter-state commerce has long since outlived its usefulness.

Financial operations. In the limited space at our disposal, we can treat only briefly the important features of the financial operations of the Tobacco Trust. From its inception to the present time centralized control has been achieved through direct ownership, either of the tangible property of the absorbed concerns or of its voting stocks. The five original concerns of the American Tobacco Company received pro-rata, in return for the property they surrendered, stocks of the new company. In

[1] *Cf.* U. S. *vs.* E. C. Knight Co., 158 W. S., 1.

[2] *Report of Commissioner of Corporations*, Dec., 1904, pp. 46–47.

the subsequent process of assimilation each plant was purchased outright and paid for partly in cash and partly with newly issued stock of the purchasing Company. Frequently, however, the Trust purchased merely a majority share of the voting stock of the particular company which it desired to control. Up to 1898 all the property of the Trust was owned and controlled by a single corporation, the American Tobacco Company. In that year was organized the Continental Tobacco Company, which owned and controlled all the plug interests formerly held by the American Tobacco Company as well as the new plants absorbed. The two companies were united by a common president, Mr. J. B. Duke, and by the American Tobacco Company holding $30,000,000 common stock of the Continental issue. In 1901 these companies were combined through the organization of a security-holding company of New Jersey, The Consolidated Tobacco Company, which issued $157,844,600 bonds in exchange for all the stocks and bonds of the two united corporations. Mr. Duke was president of the new holding corporation. Under this arrangement the former owners of property in either of the two companies now held instead certificates (bonds) of a holding corporation, which bonds were secured by the property of the individual companies. In 1904 a reorganization occurred transforming the holding company into the present American Tobacco Company, an ordinary corporation, which owns or controls directly the property of all the concerns that at one time or another passed into the control of the Trust. While its history has been comparatively free from the more conspicuous features of high finance, the insiders of the Tobacco Trust, as we shall presently see, have more than once played the game unfairly.

For instance, in 1901, when the American Tobacco

Company and the Continental were taken over by the Consolidated, the stockholders in the former companies were persuaded to exchange their stock for four per cent bonds of the holding company. The exchange of stocks for bonds was made on the assumption that the real earning power of the American stock was eight per cent and the Continental four per cent. Immediately after the consolidation took place, the common stock in these companies, which were now in the hands of the Consolidated, paid respectively ten and thirteen per cent in 1902 and twelve and sixteen per cent in 1903. This made possible a twenty per cent dividend in 1902 and 1903 on the $30,000,000 common stock of the Consolidated, which, of course, was held by the shrewd insiders who manouvered the game. The holders of common stock were fleeced by a concealment of the real earning power of the American and Continental companies. In 1904, when a reorganization again occurred, the voting power of the new American Tobacco Company was restricted to holders of common stock, of which only $40,000,000 was issued; the entire issue of capital stock and bonds being at that time $251,710,000. This common stock, which was not offered to the general investing public, has been paying at the rate of twenty per cent per annum.

Frequent manipulation of tobacco stock for speculative purposes confirms the opinion that the earnings of the Trust magnates are by no means confined to actual business profits. During the struggle of 1893, with the National Cigarette and Tobacco Company for the control of the cigarette market, common stock dropped from 127 in January to 43 in July; preferred stock falling in the same ratio. In anticipation, however, of the absorption of the "National," the insiders of the American bought up its stock when it was very low and profited by its subsequent rise. In December of 1895, with a large surplus on hand, the directors of the American Tobacco Company announced that quarterly dividends on common stock would be passed, which caused stocks to tumble from 91 to 63. The entire dividend would have amounted to only $537,000, whereas the reported surplus was $8,600,000. That there was something "shady" behind this was confirmed by certain doubtful stock manipulations which followed.[1] When stock was down to 71 in March it was bought up again by insiders who anticipated the rise occasioned by a two per cent dividend in April, 1896 which brought the stock up to 91. With stock as low as 130 in December, 1898, the Standard Oil interests entered the field and bought a large voting share. In April of 1899 a one hundred per cent stock dividend was declared and stock rose in May to 229. These are but a few of the many instances where the interests of the general investing public have been sacrificed by those in control of the Trust. In many instances greater publicity of accounts would have made such questionable financiering, if not impossible, at least more difficult.

Judged by the rate of dividends paid, the Tobacco Trust has been eminently successful. (See Appendix Table I.) On its preferred stock the American Tobacco Company paid eight per cent from 1890 to 1901. During the same period the common stock averaged nine per cent. From 1898 to 1901 the Continental paid seven per cent on its preferred stock, although it paid nothing on its common. From 1902 to 1904 dividends on American and Continental common averaged respectively eleven and fourteen and one-half per cent

[1] *Cf. Commercial and Financial Chronicle*, vol. 61, 1063 (Dec. 14, 1895). *Cf.* also N. Y. *Tribune*, Dec. 8, 1895.

annually. Since the organization of the new American Tobacco Company in 1904, preferred stock has paid six per cent and common stock twenty per cent (including the ten per cent extra dividend declared annually; the regular dividend is two and one-half per cent quarterly). This represents the earnings derived for the most part from the manufacture and sale of plug, chewing and smoking tobacco, cigarettes and snuff.

All of the Trust enterprises have not been equally successful. The Havana Tobacco Company,[1] for instance, has never paid any dividends on its common stock of $30,000,000, pointing to a heavy over-capitalization. The American Cigar Company, through which the Trust directs its domestic cigar trade, has likewise failed to pay any dividend on its common stock of $10,000,000, of which about $7,000,000 is held by the American Tobacco Company.[2] It is not unlikely that the common stock in each of these companies represents some of the inflated, watered, value of these corporations. The United Cigar Stores Company has paid on the average annually seven per cent on its stock. The American Snuff Company has earned ten per cent on its common stock, which is quoted regularly above 200.

In Table "IV" (Appendix) is presented a summary of the financial situation of the present American Tobacco Company. At the close of 1905 the outstanding stock and bonds were $238,070,750, of which only $40,000,000

[1] The total earnings for the year ending 1906, after paying deficiencies of previous years, were only $477,243, a little over one per cent on capital investment. This stock has been quoted as low as 10 and only rarely at 30.

[2] The net earnings, however, in 1906 amounted to $2,332,379, or 100 per cent more than the earnings of 1905. The earnings in 1906 were equivalent to a five per cent income on total stock and bonds ($40,000,000).

was common stock. The fixed interest charges on bonds and preferred stock were $10,593,323, whereas the earnings for the year were $25,212,285, of which $8,048,480 was devoted to the dividends on common stock, which received twenty per cent for the year. From this it appears that from the point of view of earnings the Tobacco Trust is under-capitalized. If its earnings were capitalized on a six per cent basis, the value of the stock, that is, the real capitalization, would approximate $400,-000,000. This includes the value of the property of subsidiary companies to the extent that the latter are controlled by, and contribute earnings to, the American Tobacco Company (the Trust). If we add to the above $400,000,000 that part of the property of the subsidiary companies not owned but controlled by the Trust, the total approximates $450,000,000. The entire capitalization of the subsidiary companies is in round figures about $200,000,000, of which about seventy-five per cent is owned directly by the Trust, leaving only $50,000,000 in the hands of outside interests, but not beyond the control of the Trust. In 1904 the issued and floating capitalization of the parent and subsidiary companies was estimated by Mr. Moody at $500,000,000.[1] This estimate is partially vitiated by the fact that no allowance was made for duplication of values arising from the relation between the parent and subsidiary companies. If we assume that this allowance has been offset by the increased ownership of property by the Trust since 1904, then $500,000,000 capitalization may not to-day be far from the mark.

The meagreness of the financial reports issued by the Trust prevents any positive prediction regarding its future. Barring serious industrial depressions and legal diffi-

[1] *Cf. The Truth About the Trusts*, pp. 96, 97.

culties, the Trust seems likely to expand rather than contract its activities. That the cigar industry will in the near future come as completely under the control of the Trust as are the other branches of the tobacco industry seems very probable. Before that is realized, however, is it too rash to hope for some effective control and regulation of the Trust by federal law? Until now the agitation and protest against the Trust has come mainly from those engaged within and directly affected by the industry, as growers of leaf, manufacturers, jobbers, the retailers and the investing public. Presently we may hear from the consumer.

In our study of the Tobacco Trust it has been our aim to point out the following facts: first, that the Trust has been most successful in those branches of the industry in which concentration in manufacturing had been carried to the point of relative maximum efficiency in production; second, that the economies in production and distribution affected by the Trust, although appreciable, were not the predominant or decisive factors in its successful development; third, that it is to superior methods of competition in the marketing of goods that it owes its present position, which methods have been efficient because ruinous to small individual competitors; fourth, that its monopoly power consists not merely in raising prices of finished products arbitrarily and in depressing the price of raw material, but in its ability to reserve for itself a large portion of the tobacco trade by making it very difficult for competitors to enter the field; fifth, that those most directly interested in the promotion and regulation of the Trust affairs have frequently profited by using their *inside* information in stock manipulation and speculation.

APPENDIX—Table I.

FINANCIAL SUMMARY OF AMERICAN TOBACCO COMPANY (1891–1904).

	1891.	1892.	1893.	1894.	1895.	1896.	1897.	1898.	1899.	1900.	1901.	1902.	1903.
Assets [1]	$32,330,393	$36,171,390	$37,168,253	$38,700,596	$40,782,607	$41,153,714	$42,289,236	$62,297,755	$77,075,543	$79,933,253	$91,123,613	$88,434,337	$86,040,261
Capital stock (outstanding) [2]	[3] 29,835,000	29,835,000	29,835,000	29,830,000	[4] 30,280,000	[5] 33,597,000	[6] 33,597,000	[7] 38,560,000	[8] 71,524,490	[9] 71,514,490	[10] 71,514,490	[11] 68,500,000	68,500,000
Earnings	4,331,995	4,739,301	4,334,467	5,069,416	3,971,521	3,593,197	4,179,460	4,957,804	5,202,384	6,303,198	6,647,114	7,450,575	8,664,185
Dividend on preferred	8 p. c.	8 p. c.	8 p. c.	8 p. c.	8 p. c.	8 p. c.	8 p. c.	8 p. c.	8 p. c.	8 p. c.	8 p. c.	8 p. c.	8 p. c.
On common stock	12 p. c.	12 p. c.	12 p. c.	12 p. c.	[12] 9 p. c.	[13] 9 p. c. +	8 p. c.	8 p. c.	[14] 6½ p. c. +	6 p. c.	6 p. c.	10 p. c.	12 p. c.
Surplus (accumulative)	$2,495,393	$4,107,895	$5,333,062	$7,198,290	$8,600,371	$5,884,549	$7,447,849	[15] $22,557,689	[16] $2,575,430	[17] $4,308,094	[17] $6,384,317	$7,204,609	$8,209,304

[1] Includes real estate, plants, leaf, trade-marks, good will, etc. [2] Authorized issue in 1891 was $35,000,000. [3] $17,900,000 C., $11,935,000 P. [4] $18,283,000 C., $12,117,000 P. [5] $17,900,000 C., $3,560,000 C. S., $11,935,000 P., $182,000 P. S. [6] Same as 1896. [7] $21,000,000 C., $3,560,000 C. S., $14,000,000 P. [8] $54,500,000 C., $3,024,000 C. S., $14,000,000 P. [9] $54,500,000 C., $3,014,000 C. S., $14,000,000 P. [10] Same as 1900. [11] $54,500,000 C., $14,000,000 P. [12] Last quarter (3 per cent) was passed, see p. 134. [13] 9 per cent cash and 20 per cent stock dividend. [14] 6½ per cent cash and 100 per cent stock dividend. [15] Including cash and stock received from sale of plug interests, etc., "Continental Tob. Co." [16] $21,000,000 taken from previous surplus to pay 100 per cent stock dividend. [17] Does not include surplus in subsidiary companies.

TABLE II.

SUMMARY OF CONTINENTAL TOBACCO COMPANY (1899–1904).

	1899.	1900.	1901.	1902.	1903.
Assets	$99,928,017	$104,378,952	$111,621,613	$119,820,442	$120,606,180
Capital stock [1]	100,000,000	100,000,000	100,000,000	100,000,000	100,000,000
Earnings	[2] 2,032,756	4,480,858	7,600,740	11,776,934	12,756,784
Dividend on preferred	[4] 3½ p. c.	7 p. c.	7 p. c.	7 p. c.	7 p. c.
On common stock	0	0	2 p. c.	[5] 13 p. c.	16 p. c.
Surplus (accumulative)	$323,195	1,384,931	4,589,627	$5,597,446	$8,119,732

[1] Original capitalization authorized Dec. 9, 1898) was $75,000,000, but increased to $100,000,000 April 21, 1899. [2] $48,844,600 C., $48,846,600 P. [3] Active business did not begin until middle of 1899. [4] Represents earnings for only one-half year (note 3). [5] After 1901, common stock was held by insiders of Consolidated Tob. Co.

TABLE III.

SUMMARY OF CONSOLIDATED TOBACCO COMPANY (1901–1904).

	1901.	1902.	1903.
Assets [1]	2	$196,581,917	$214,941,041
Stocks [3] and bonds [4]	[5] $186,000,000	186,593,400	[6] 197,378,200
Earnings	2	13,241,466	16,359,124
Dividend on bonds	2	4 p. c.	4 p. c.
Common stock	2	20 p. c.	20 p. c.
Surplus	2	[7] $950,216	$985,913

[1] Stocks of A. T. C. and Continental, as well as stock of foreign companies. [2] Consolidation took place June, 1901. No annual report till 1902. [3] Common stock kept by insiders, never offered to public. [4] 4 per cent bonds issued in exchange for stock of A. T. C. and Continental. [5] $30,000,000 C., $156,000,000 B. [6] $40,000,000 C., $157,378,200 B. [7] Exclusive of the Consolidated share of surplus of A. T. C. and "Cont." and subsidiary companies.

TABLE IV.

FINANCIAL SUMMARY OF NEW AMERICAN TOBACCO COMPANY (1904–1906).

	1904.	1905.
Assets [1]	$293,620,115	$274,361,060
	78,689,100 B4	63,489,100 B4
	56,090,400 B6	55,650,150 B6
	78,689,100 P6	78,689,100 P6
	40,242,400 C	40,242,400 C
Stocks [2] and bonds	$251,710,000	$238,070,750
Earnings [3]	22,304,696	25,212,285
Dividends on 6 per cent bonds	[4]841,356	3,332,413
On 4 per cent bonds	786,891	2,539,564
Preferred stock	6 p. c.	6 p. c.
Earnings	[4]1,180,337	4,721,346
Common stock	[4]0	[6]20 p. c.
Earnings	....	8,048,480
Surplus	[5]29,518,879	25,685,961

[1] Assets in 1904 represented by the following:

Real estate, machinery, trade-mark, good will, etc.	$139,604,437
Leaf tobacco, and other stock on hand	24,405,452
Stocks in foreign companies	23,925,420
Stocks in domestic companies	55,532,890
Cash	8,028,236
Commissions prepaid	600,964
Bills and accounts received	41,522,716
Total	$293,620,115

[2] Stocks—Authorized issue of common stock was $100,000,000.

Authorized issue of preferred stock was $80,000,000.

Four per cent bonds are payable 1944.

Six per cent bonds are payable 1951.

Bonds and preferred stock of new A. T. C. issued in exchange for bonds and preferred shares of "Consolidated" and old A. T. C. and "Continental."

Common stock issued in exchange for "Common" of Consolidated, which were held by insiders.

[3] Earnings—The $22,304,696 represented the total earnings for the calendar year, of all the constituent, merged companies.

[4] From October 1 to December 31, 1904 inclusive.

[5] Total surplus taken over from merged companies. In 1905, $9,988,990 was taken from surplus to retire $15,200,000 4 per cent bonds when the market price of the latter stood at 65.

[6] Dividend on common—2½ per cent is regular quarterly dividend, but a 10 per cent yearly extra was paid in 1905. In 1906 a 12½ per cent extra dividend was paid besides the regular 10 per cent dividend for the year.

CHAPTER V

Labor Conditions in the Tobacco Industry

Because of the heterogeneous elements in the organization of the tobacco industry it is impossible to make any broad generalizations concerning the conditions of the workers as a whole. The rate of wages, hours of labor and general conditions of employment in the manufacture of plug, chewing tobacco, smoking tobacco, snuff and machine-made cigarettes, are very different from those conditions that obtain in the cigar industry. In the manufacture of the former products, machinery, operated by unskilled labor, has played the important rôle, whereas, in the cigar industry, skilled hand labor has been, and is yet, the determining factor in production. This fundamental difference in the technical processes of production results in the division of the workers, as respects their condition, into two classes. Moreover, within the cigar industry itself, which is in a transition stage between the handicraft and the machine system of production, there is a diversity of conditions and problems. One of the interesting aspects of the labor problem in the industry is the proof afforded of this vital relation between the status of the workers and the character of the technical processes that they are called upon to perform.

The successful application of comparatively automatic machinery in the manufacture of plug, chewing and smoking tobacco, snuff and cigarettes has made possible the exploitation, not merely of unskilled male labor, but of female and child labor as well. The greater part of the work consists in tending and feeding the machines. Where skill is required, as in wrapping and in making twists and spun rolls, only few hands are employed. Fully one half of the entire working force are women and children, receiving, as we shall see later, wretchedly low wages. It is in order to take advantage of the constant and large supply of low-grade city labor, that the tobacco factories have been located in large industrial centers.[1] As competition among this class of laborers is very intense, wages and hours of labor are decidedly unsatisfactory.

The situation of the tobacco workers has been further aggravated by the concentration of the manufacturing interests in the hands of the Trust. In its relation to its employees, this gigantic corporation has acted without a soul; but more than that, it has denied the workers even a body. For by refusing to bargain with organized labor collectively, and by adopting a generally hostile attitude toward organizations, the Trust disrupted the labor union in 1895, and since its reorganization has been successful in keeping it weak and inefficient. When the Trust has not antagonized the union directly, it has done so indirectly by taking advantage of its position as a large individual purchaser of labor, in a market of many unorganized laborers. In this situation, where the parties concerned have such unequal power, the terms of the labor contract are bound to be unfair to the weaker party, that is the laborer.

Before considering in detail the actual economic status of the tobacco workers, let us first analyze briefly their

[1] *Supra*, p. 97.

composition. Since 1880 the general tendency has been toward the displacement of child by adult female labor, the proportion of adult male laborers remaining almost stationary. Of the entire working force, the percentage of children under sixteen has declined since 1880 from twenty-one to nine per cent, while adult female labor increased in the same period from thirty-two to thirty-eight per cent. Women and children together comprised, in 1905, forty-seven per cent.[1] In connection with these figures it should be borne in mind that, even under modern sanitary conditions, which do not always obtain, the tobacco trade is dangerous to the health of the workers, many of whom die from tuberculosis.

With respect to the employment of child labor, North Carolina is the chief offender, having engaged in her factories, in 1905, no less than 1,134 children under sixteen years of age, which is almost twenty per cent of the total number of workers employed in her tobacco factories.[2] A society mindful of the welfare of its individuals would forbid the employment in tobacco factories, not only of children but also of females under twenty-one years of age. In the following table is presented the number of tobacco workers distinguished according to sex and age, since 1860:[3]

Number of Tobacco Workers Employed, by Sex and Age Groups, Since 1860 in the United States.

	1860.	1870.	1880.	1890.	1900.	1905	Per cent for 1905.	Per cent of increase or decrease since 1860.
Total	18,859	21,799	32,756	29,790	29,161	23,990	100	— 28
Males	13,869	19,588	14,886	14,942	14,124	12,721	53	— 9
Females	2,990	5,179	10,776	10,564	11,590	9,127	38	+105
Children under 16.	[4]	6,032	7,094	4,284	3,447	3,447	9	— 42[4]

[1] *Cf. Census of Manufactures, 1905, United States, Bulletin 37*, p. 91.

[2] *Cf. Census of Manufactures, 1905, North Carolina, Bulletin 39*, p. 18.

[3] *U. S. Census Bulletin, No. 197* (1902), *Manufactures of Tobacco*, p. 24; also *Census of Manufactures, 1905, United States*, p. 91.

[4] Not reported separately until 1870.

Wages in the industry are incredibly low.[1] In an ordinary tobacco factory wages range from forty cents per day for strippers or stemmers, up to one dollar and twenty-five cents per day for lump-makers, nip-wrappers, potters and shipping clerks. Pickers (those selecting the leaf) earn about eighty cents per day, and machine operators one dollar per day. In a typical Virginia factory, employing one hundred and forty hands, the average wage per day is ninety cents, making an annual income of $247.50 for two hundred and seventy-five days of labor.[2] In Northern factories, where industrial opportunities are greater, wages are, in general, twenty-five per cent higher. On the basis of the data presented in the reports of the state bureaus of labor, and using whenever possible a weighted average, the annual income of a tobacco worker in ten different states is given in the following table:

ANNUAL WAGE OF TOBACCO WORKERS, MEN, WOMEN, CHILDREN.

	Adult Male.	Adult Female.	Children under 16.	Principal Manufacturing Centers.
North Carolina	$240	$154	$123	Durham & Winston.
Virginia	255	180	113	Richmond.
Kentucky	320	215	120	Louisville.
Ohio	375	255	135	Cincinnati.
Maryland	408	242	116	Baltimore.
Missouri	428	370	370	St. Louis.
New Jersey	450	350	200	Jersey City.
Michigan	475	263	190	Detroit.
Illinois	500	270	160	Chicago.
New York	528	324	169	New York.

[1] We refer here to all branches except cigars, hand-made cigarettes, and hand-made stogies.

[2] *Cf. Fifth Annual Report of the Bureau of Labor Statistics of Virginia*, 1902, pp. 73-81.

In the first six states, of which all except Ohio are Southern, and which manufacture about seventy-five per cent of the entire output of the country, the average annual wage for adult males is $330, for females $236, for children $162. In the four Northern states, which produce less than twenty-five per cent of the entire product, the average wage is $488 for adult males, $300 for women, and $180 for children. This low income has been constant, or nearly so, for over a decade.

For this small reward the tobacco worker toils from nine to ten hours per day, for only in exceptional instances, where the labor union is strong, does the eight-hour day prevail. The general average for the week is from fifty-four to sixty hours. Although the work does not require much intense physical exertion, it is monotonous and very confining. The sickly, yellow complexion of the average tobacco worker is the most convincing evidence of the devitalizing character of the work.

Where the tobacco workers have been able to effect a strong organization, their conditions have been slightly improved, not only with respect to the hours of labor, but also with respect to wages. The Tobacco Workers' International Union has not, however, been successful in extending its activities to factories operated by the Trust, which employs over seventy-five per cent of the entire labor force in the industry. In that part of the industry still uncontrolled by the Trust the Union owes no small degree of its present power and position to a willingness and desire of the independent manufacturers to utilize the Union label in their fight against the Trust. To the extent that he pays higher wages, the independent manufacturer looks upon the Union label as an investment. For him it is one form of advertisement, the value of which he capitalizes to offset the relatively higher wage.

Depending, as it does, not entirely upon its own innate strength, but partly upon the peculiar and probably temporary support of the independent manufacturer, the Union's position is therefore a precarious one.

Apart from the hostile opposition of the Trust[1] the Union must face other serious obstacles in the way of an efficient and complete organization. There is, first of all, a large number of women and children to deal with, almost fifty per cent of the workers in the trade. This has always been one of the serious drawbacks to organization among the workers. Moreover, the low standard of wages and working conditions in the industry is not likely to attract a very intelligent class of workers. To these obstacles must be added the problem of negro labor, which is employed extensively in Southern factories.

The present Tobacco Workers' International Union was organized in 1895 and is affiliated with the American Federation of Labor. Although it enrolled, in the period from 1895 to 1900, no less than twenty-five thousand members, the Union had, in 1901, only four thousand members.[2] The large falling off was due to the absorption of independent factories by the Trust. In the face of these many obstacles, the Union deserves much credit for organizing, as it has, from ten to fifteen per cent of the workers. In spite of the small membership fee, (ten cents weekly), the Union is able to pay both sick and death benefits. Provision is also made for a strike fund; those on strike receiving three dollars per week. We pass by the details of its organization, since we shall consider at length in this chapter the cigar

[1] *Cf. Report of the Industrial Commission*, vol. vii, pp. 399, 405.

[2] *Cf. Report of Industrial Commission*, vol. xvii; *cf.* also *Tobacco Workers' Journal*, Oct., 1900, pp. 17–18.

makers' union, after which it is modelled.[1] In some of the largest independent factories in the country the Tobacco Workers' Union has succeeded in establishing a minimum wage and the eight-hour day.[2]

The Cigar Industry. To understand the labor conditions in the cigar trade, we must have in mind the general character of the industry. In the manufacture of cigars, except in the production of cheap scrap-filler goods, the "bunches" of which are shaped by machinery, the amount of hand skill required is sufficient to check the supply of labor, thus influencing the rate of wages favorably to the workers.[3] The Cigar Makers' Union imposes, as a condition of membership, a three years' apprenticeship which though considered by many too long a period, is some indication of the character of the work. One year apprenticeship may be safely regarded as the minimum required in the manufacture of a mold cigar, and five years for a hand-made cigar.

Another factor favorable to the skilled worker is the ready opportunity of becoming an independent employer. This alternative is made possible by two reasons: first, not only is little or no fixed capital needed, but such circulating capital as is necessary can easily be secured on credit; moreover, the circulating capital, consisting of leaf on hand and outstanding stock,

[1] The headquarters of the Tobacco Workers' International Union are located at Louisville, Kentucky, corner of Third and Main Streets. Mr. Henry Fischer is President of the Union, and E. Lewis Evans, Secretary-Treasurer.

[2] Among others, the following factories have been unionized: The U. S. Tobacco Co., Richmond, Va.; the Globe Tobacco Co., Detroit, Mich.; Larus Bros., Richmond, Va.; the Monarch Tobacco Works, Louisville, Ky.; Leopold Miller & Sons, N. Y. City.

[3] For a description of the technical processes in production of cigars, *Cf. supra*, pp. 82, 83.

is equivalent to only about five hundred dollars per employee; and secondly, the organization of the retail trade on a petty and personal basis affords a market to the small manufacturer for the disposal of his goods. That these conditions of production and distribution, discussed at length in our chapter on manufactures, are not hypothetical may be seen from the situation that obtains in New York state at the present time. Out of 1,412 factories inspected, over fifty-eight per cent of the employers, besides working themselves, engaged only one apprentice and one journeyman; sixty-six worked without any hired help whatsoever. In 1905 about eighteen per cent of the entire number of cigar makers were engaged in factories having an annual output of only twenty thousand dollars or less, which is equivalent to the product of four skilful workmen.[1]

Both of these conditions, the skill required in making cigars and the general character of production and distribution in the industry, have made possible a third factor, which likewise operates in the interest of the workers, namely, effective organization among the employees. The Cigar Makers' Union has been, in fact, one of the remarkably strong labor organizations in this country in the last fifty years, and is very largely responsible for the present standard of wages and hours of labor enjoyed by the workers. Of its history, organization and achievements we shall have more to say later. We wish here merely to refer to it as one of the several factors which have helped to maintain living conditions among the workers.

In spite of what has been said, the wages of the cigar makers are comparatively low. Except in rare instances,

[1] *Cf. U. S. Census of Manufactures, 1905, New York*, p. 45.

as in the case of apprentices, strippers and machine operators, the piece-wage system prevails. In non-union and open shops the rate of wages varies from five to seven dollars a thousand cigars, (bunching and rolling); in union shops the scale ranges from eight to ten dollars per thousand cigars complete.[1] This is the rate for mold-made cigars; the rate for hand-made cigars is about twenty-five per cent higher. Of mold cigars, the average cigar maker can produce about forty per hour, bunching and rolling, or roughly speaking, three hundred per day for eight hours' labor, (the period in union shops) and four hundred in a ten hour day, which obtains in non-union shops. In both cases the wages approximate twelve dollars per week, the union man working forty-five hours and the non-union man from fifty-four to sixty hours. This is the wage for the man of average speed. Of course, the more adept the worker, the higher are his wages. It is not uncommon for a union man to earn from fifteen to twenty dollars per week on mold cigars, but this is the exception rather than the rule. Moreover, the work is unsteady and consequently the annual income is to that extent reduced. In most shops, and especially in small ones, the period of unemployment averages two months in the year. The total number engaged in the trade, including packers and strippers, approximates 125,000.[2]

[1] The rate in any single shop varies according to the size and shape and style of the cigar. A five-inch cigar pays more than a four-and-a-half-inch. A perfecto shape pays more than a straight cigar, a long-filler more than a scrap cigar.

[2] According to the *Census of Manufactures, 1905, U. S.*, the number employed in the cigar and cigarette industry combined was reported as 137,000. The number of cigarette makers could not have exceeded 12,000, plus the number of cigar makers of whom the census took no cognizance. Of the 125,000 engaged in the cigar trade about 100,000 are bona-fide cigar makers.

According to the most recent figures of the United States Bureau of Labor reports,[1] wages in the cigar industry for 1905 for bunchers and rollers were $11.44 per week for fifty-two hours' labor, the average wage per hour being $0.22. The annual income for forty-four weeks would be five hundred dollars. This was the wage for mold work in 1905, when wages were higher than they have been for some years. This same bulletin puts the wages in New York, Boston, Chicago, Cleveland, Detroit, and Philadelphia at fifteen dollars per week, or six hundred dollars for the year. According to the data in the reports of the state bureaus of labor the wages in the three leading cigar states are as follows:

Annual Wages in Cigar Trade (For Males).

New York State............	$592	In union shops only (five year average).
Ohio	517	In union and non-union shops (four year average).
Pennsylvania	400	In union and non-union shops (for single year).

For these three states the weighted average annual wage was five hundred dollars. The low wage in Pennsylvania is due to the exploitation of labor under the domestic or household system of production. In Tampa and Key West, Florida, where most of our Havana hand-made cigars are produced, wages average six hundred and thirty dollars per year. On the other hand, female operators of bunch-breaking machines receive from five to seven dollars per week, averaging three hundred dollars per year for forty-three weeks' work. Under the piece-wage system these operators earn thirteen cents per

[1] *Cf. U. S. Bureau of Labor, Bulletin 65*, p. 57.

hour, and their work extends through fifty-four hours per week.[1]

The difference in wages paid in Northern and Southern factories is very marked. In the South Atlantic division, excepting Florida, males on mold work receive seventeen cents per hour, and female operators nine cents per hour; whereas, in the North Atlantic division males receive twenty-three cents on mold work, and female operators thirteen cents per hour.[2] This variation in income is attributable not alone to the quality of the work produced, nor to the difference in the standard of living, but partly to the lack of organization among the workers.

The effect of organization upon the rate of wages is also noticeable in comparing the income of cigar makers in different localities where unionism is strong and weak. In Boston, which is the recognized leading union city in the country, the average rate of wage is forty-two cents per hour, as compared with thirty-two cents for New York City, where unionism is confessedly weaker than in Boston. Contrast also the yearly income of union cigar makers in New York State, where organization is relatively strong and union men receive $592, with Pennsylvania where the union is very weak and the annual income is only $397; in New York City the rate for bunching and rolling is thirty-two cents per hour, compared with twenty-four cents in Philadelphia. In Binghampton, New York, where many non-union shops are located, the scale is seven dollars per thousand cigars, whereas, in Rochester, New York, for the same grade of work the wage is ten dollars per thousand. In large industrial centers where, owing to the influx of a large

[1] *Cf. U. S. Bureau of Labor*, *Bulletin 65*, p. 57 (1906).

[2] *Ibid.*, pp. 55-61.

supply of foreign labor, we naturally expect to find wages lower than in inland towns and villages, the reverse is usually the case wherever unionism is strong. Take, for instance, Massachusetts in which the average yearly income, in 1905, was $660; in Boston where the union is exceptionally efficient, the income is $825; whereas, for eighteen towns in the rest of the state (including such places as Springfield, Lowell, Lynn, Fall River and Worcester) where the workers are less powerfully organized, the average was only $640.[1] This is not due to a difference in the cost of living, for in New York, where the cost of living is as high as in any part of the country, but where the union is not very strongly organized, wages are lower than in Boston and smaller cities, where labor is well organized. In fact, the union, in poorly organized centers, is forced to permit its members to work below the regular union scale that obtains in other more strongly unionized cities.

This double standard of wages, one for union and the other for non-union shops, prevails within the confines of any single city; usually ten dollars per thousand in the former, and seven or eight dollars in the latter. In general, it may be said that the wages in union shops are from ten to twenty per cent in advance of non-union shops: or, putting it in another, more realistic way, the non-union worker must toil fifty-five hours per week to earn what the union man receives for forty-five hours' labor. Why, then, it may be asked, do not all workers seek jobs in union shops? For two reasons: first, they have frequently learned the trade in less time than is required by the union for apprenticeship, and conse-

[1] *Cf. Census of Manufactures, 1906, Massachusetts, Bulletin 53*, pp. 54-58.

quently are ineligible to membership; secondly, some workers by remaining outside the union and working below the union scale of wages, or by working overtime, more than eight hours per day, can earn a larger net income than by submitting to union regulations.

Society is indebted to the Cigar Makers' Union for having been the first organization in America successfully to enforce the eight-hour day, which is especially important in the cigar industry because of the unhealthful character of the work. The number of deaths due to tuberculosis has been shockingly high, but is being constantly reduced through the Union's efforts to improve sanitary conditions and by providing "benefits" for its sick members.[1]

In spite of all efforts on the part of the Union and the general public, child labor has not been eradicated from this dangerous trade. On the contrary, it has greatly increased since 1890. According to the latest census figures[2] the number of children under sixteen employed in cigar and cigarette factories in 1890 was 3,334; in 1900 there were 3,587, and in 1905 there were 5,274, an increase since 1890 of nearly sixty per cent. While it is impossible to ascertain accurately whether this increase has occurred in cigar or cigarette factories (since the two are reported jointly in this census report), it is more than likely that it came in the cigar trade, since this industry has flourished with won-

[1] The Union's vital statistics show the following deaths from consumption and lung trouble of one kind or another: In 1890, 60 per cent; in 1895, 43 per cent; in 1900, 35 per cent. Longevity among union members in the same years was as follows: 1890, 37 years; 1895, 39 years; 1900, 43 years. *Cf. Report of the President of the International Cigar Makers' Union*, 1901.

[2] *Cf. Census of Manufactures, 1905, United States, Bulletin 57*, p. 91.

derful rapidity in the last decade. The Cigar Makers' Union is conducting a crusade against goods made by child labor in Trust factories, where boys and girls are employed not only in "stripping" (removing the tough midrib from leaf), but also in operating cigar machinery. The number of women engaged in that part of the cigar and cigarette industry reported in the 1905 census[1] was 57,174, of which probably 15,000 are in the cigar industry.

From what has already been said, it must be apparent that the conditions of the working class in the cigar industry have been largely influenced, if not shaped, by the Cigar Makers' Union. This is all the more remarkable in view of the fact that at no time were more than one-half of the entire labor force enrolled in the Union. In April, 1906, union membership was 45,784, which is approximately about thirty-five per cent of the entire trade.[2] It is one of the oldest labor organizations in the country, and in many important aspects is modelled after the English type of trade union. A local organization existed in Cincinnati as far back as 1841; a state (New York) convention of locals was held in 1854, and the first national convention, at which the present union had its birth, met in 1864. Into its historical development, however, it is not our purpose to enter.[3] We shall confine our study to a description and analysis of a few of

[1] *Census of Manufactures, 1905, United States*, p. 91.

[2] *Cf. Cigar Makers' Official Journal*, Apr. 15, 1906.

[3] For a historical account of the rise of the Cigar Makers' Union, *cf.* Adolph Strasser's sketch in *The Labor Movement*, by Geo. E. McNeill; *cf.* also *Report of the Industrial Commission*, vol. xvii, but especially an article by T. A. Glocker on the "Structure of the Cigar Makers' Union," pub. in *Studies in American Trade Unions*, edited by Hollander & Barnett, 1906.

its important features only in so far as they shed some light on the present and future problems of unionism.

After forty years' experience the Cigar Makers' International Union has developed one of the most democratic and efficient labor organizations in our country. It is a federation of five hundred comparatively autonomous local unions. Each local organization is thoroughly democratic and self-governing in affairs which concern merely its own interests. Its administration is guided by an elective and salaried secretary-treasurer, and a non-salaried but elective executive board. The secretary has the supervision over membership rolls, payment of dues, assessments, fines, etc., and the dispensation of "benefits" to members. The secretary is assisted in minor matters by shop collectors, invested by the local union with the power of collecting dues and fines and reporting conditions in their respective shops. The secretary reports monthly to the international president at Chicago. The executive board acts in an advisory and judicial capacity over matters relating to the local. The powers and duties of the locals will be discussed later. Each local is governed by its own by-laws and rules, besides that of the constitution of the international union.

At the head of the international organization stands a president-secretary, elected every five years by a referendum vote of all the members of all locals. As secretary he conducts all correspondence between locals and the international. As president he is the executive organ for the enforcement of all national legislation. He authorizes payments of "benefits," equalizes the funds of the various locals, levies fines, suspends and expels members. He also appoints label agitators and financial and strike agents, who report regularly to him. In jurisdiction disputes, involving an interpretation of the constitution, the president acts as a judicial arbiter.

Above and along with the president, however, stands an executive board consisting of seven vice-presidents, in addition to the president, and a treasurer, all of whom, like the president, are elected by a referendum vote every five years. To the executive board all members and locals can appeal from the decisions of the president. The executive board authorizes the levying of assessments for replenishing funds, grants charters to locals, passes upon executive appointments, and exercises final jurisdiction over strikes involving less than twenty-five members.

The final authority, however, not only in judicial matters, but also in legislation, rests in the entire membership acting through the locals. As a last resort, any decision of consequence can be carried to the entire membership, through a referendum vote. Likewise, all national legislation is effected by the direct vote of the locals, through a referendum vote. In matters of legislation, the power of initiation also resides with the local body, and in some cases is vested in the members acting individually. The constitution of the international union is amended, when occasion demands, by this process of the initiative and referendum. Having discovered that this was economically the cheaper method of making laws, no international convention has been held since 1896. A fine is imposed on all members who do not avail themselves of the opportunity to vote for international officials. In the last election, 1906, seventy-five per cent of the entire membership voted; on ordinary legislation, however, less than one-half cast their ballots.

As regards the form of organization, therefore, the Cigar Makers' Union is highly democratic. Very little final or arbitrary power is vested in the hands of the international officers. On all important questions, the members or locals have at their disposal the power of agitating, initiating and legislating all measures. The central body is merely a convenient and expeditious means through which the members express their will freely and democratically. It is in the best sense, therefore, a self-governing body.

An efficient federation, however, always implies a surrender of some powers by the local units to the central governing body of the federation, in this instance, a majority of the local unions or members acting through locals. This leads us to a consideration of the division of powers between the locals and the international, which we shall discuss under three heads: regulation of finances, trade regulations, and strikes.

Members pay local dues weekly and international assessments at irregular intervals.[1] Local unions do not participate in the enjoyment of the assessments which go directly to the central headquarters, and out of which are paid the expenses of the International administration. Of the moneys collected from weekly dues, the locals are entitled to expend, on the average, about twenty per cent for their own administration expenses, etc.[2] The remaining surplus, eighty per cent, is held by the local union but is the property of the International, to be used as a fund in paying benefits to the individual members, provided for under the constitution. The local therefore acts as a financial distributing agency for the International. Should the fund of any particular local become

[1] The constitution provides for 15, 20 and 30 cent members, depending upon the amount of benefits in which they desire to participate. Of the 45,000 members, over 40,000 are 30 cent members, receiving the maximum benefits.

[2] The percentage to which they are entitled depends on the size of the membership of any particular local.

exhausted through legitimate payments, it is replenished or equalized, as it is called, from the funds of other locals that may have expended less than their pro rata amount allowed by the constitution. The sinking fund of the International, though held by the locals, is always to be at least ten dollars per capita. To-day, with a membership of forty-five thousand, the fund approximates seven hundred thousand dollars. Concerning this financial system, Mr. G. W. Perkins, president of the union, wrote, "Under this system no man could steal the funds if he wanted to, and the remarkable and gratifying feature is that we do not lose on an average two hundred dollars a year through defalcations; and the money transactions, including the balance on hand, amount to about $1,-300,000 annually."

As in fiscal affairs and policies, so also in matters pertaining to trade regulatious, the locals have conferred upon the International a stringent control. The International has prescribed for the union shops everywhere the following: (1) a uniform apprenticeship law, which requires three years' experience as one of the qualifications for admission into the union;[1] (2) a uniform minimum wage—seven dollars per thousand for the United States and six dollars for Canada;[2] (3) an eight hour working day; (4) a minimum price list for all manufacturers who use the union label; goods sold be-

[1] The International Constitution provides that an apprentice can be employed only where the manufacturer engages also a journeyman. It is left to the local, with the approval of the International, to regulate the ratio between the number of apprentices to journeymen, usually ten journeymen must be employed to permit two apprentices; fifteen for three, but never more than three.

[2] Locals are permitted to enforce a wage scale of their own above this minimum, the average being $10 per thousand.

low twenty dollars per thousand can not be labelled; (5) conditions upon which the label can be granted including the above regulations. Owing to competition between localities, these questions could not advisably be left to local unions. Without a centralized control there would be no concerted action among the workers. With few exceptions, the union enforces the "closed" shop by refusing to permit their members to work in non-union shops. An exception to this rule is made in the case of New York City factories.

The power to strike is also vested in the entire International membership rather than in the local. Should a local enter on a strike without consulting, or in defiance of, the will of the International, it can claim no financial assistance from the International organization. Practically all strikes, therefore, must be sanctioned either by the executive board or by a majority of all locals through a referendum vote. When trouble arises between employees and employers, an official statement of difficulties involved must be transmitted directly to the International president and the executive board. When less than twenty-five employees are involved, the decision of the executive board is final. Where more than twenty-five are involved, the proposition, if approved by the executive board, must be submitted to a vote of all the local unions, a majority of all the locals and two-thirds of the votes cast being necessary for final approval.[1] Should the executive board refuse in the first instance to give its approval, the particular local union or unions involved

[1] The locals vote as units, but each local has a voting power proportionate to its membership: one vote for 50 members and less, two for 50 to 100 members, three from 100 to 200, and one additional vote for every 100 additional members. A secret vote is required on all questions involving a strike.

can appeal from their decision to a vote of all the locals. The strike having been sanctioned by the International body, the men on strike receive from the International fund a benefit equivalent to five dollars per week for the first sixteen weeks and three dollars per week thereafter until the strike is terminated. With respect, therefore, to the division of power between locals and the international it may be said that the decision of questions concerning the welfare of members beyond any particular union's power is vested in the entire international membership as a whole.

This cautious and conservative procedure has been amply justified by the net results of strikes entered upon. The following table of figures indicates the final outcome of strikes for the five-year period from 1896 to 1901:[1]

STRIKES AND THEIR OUTCOME.

	Number of Difficulties.	Union Members Involved.	Number Entitled to Benefit.	Non-unionists Involved.
Successful	300	12,794	11,587	10,363
Compromised	27	652	625	946
Ended by members obtaining employment elsewhere..	61	428	421	220
Lost	79	1,738	1,440	3,024
In progress or pending final report ..	27	2,618	2,115	1,381
Pending approval..	1	14	12	
Total	495	18,244	16,206	15,934
Disapproved	36	463	451	321
Grand total......	531	18,707	16,657	16,255

About sixty per cent of the number of strikes, involving

[1] These figures are taken from the *Report of President of Cigar Makers' International Union*, Sept., 1901. While it is true generally that such figures are apt to be distorted by personal bias and the desire of the Union to make a favorable showing, it must be stated that the statistical data of this particular Union are unusually accurate and complete.

sixty-eight per cent of the workers, were successful. Even more significant is the fact that for the strikes arising from a demand for an increase of wages, one hundred and two out of one hundred and twenty-four were successful, benefiting 9,855 workers (union and non-union). Of those strikes arising from an opposition to the reduction of wages, ninety-two out of one hundred and thirty-nine were successful, benefiting thereby 7,-451 workers. The income, therefore, of over 17,000 workers was affected favorably by means of the strike. Moreover, as the growing power of the union has often made strikes unnecessary, the potential strike must be considered an asset in estimating what the union has accomplished for its members through its striking power. Judging from the amount of strike benefits paid, there has been a diminution in the number, as well as in the duration of strikes.[1] In the recent large strike of the Boston cigar makers for an increase in wages the union won a decisive victory for the 2,100 workers involved.

Because of the skill required in the trade, it is no easy matter to fill the places of the striking workmen. Moreover, we must not overlook another factor, namely, the power which the union label confers upon the organized workers, in enabling them to force concessions from manufacturers whose trade depends upon that label. For twenty years fully twenty per cent of all our domestic cigars has borne the union label.[2] No labor organization has made such splendid use of the label as has the Cigar Makers' Union of its "Blue Label." It is valuable enough to be counterfeited. Cigars bearing the union

[1] *Cf. infra*, p. 162, Table.

[2] *Cf. Eleventh Special Report of U. S. Bureau of Labor* on "Regulation and Restriction of Output," p. 584 (1904).

label are worth from three to five dollars per thousand more than non-labeled goods.

The stability, as well as the strength of the Cigar Makers' Union depends in no small degree upon its splendid system of benefits. It was Mr. Adolph Strasser who recognized, so far back as the seventies, that an efficient union looked after the welfare of its members in time of peace as well as in war. To-day this union has the most complete system of benefits of all unions in the country.[1] The following table indicates the different kinds of benefits provided for, as well as their amounts, in any single year:

SYSTEM OF BENEFITS IN CIGAR MAKERS' UNION.

Kinds.	Amount Paid.
Traveling loans	$20 at one time. After finding employment borrower must pay his debt at the rate of 10 per cent of his wages.
Out of employment	$3 per week—18 weeks (maximum) in one year—Total $54.
Sick benefit	$5 per week—13 weeks (maximum) in one year—Total $65.
Strike benefit	$5 per week—16 weeks; $3 after sixteenth week—Total for year $188.
Death benefit and permanent disability	$50 to $500 Varying with length of membership.

In such a system of benefits the worker finds an inducement not only to join, but to remain in, the union. To participate in all possible benefits, each member contributed per year, from 1900 to 1905, only $8.93, or seventeen cents per week. It is a significant fact, that in periods of depression, when union membership usually declines, the Cigar Makers' Union more than held its

[1] There is a detailed analysis of the "Benefit System of the Cigar Makers' Union," by Helen H. Sumner, in *Trades Unions and Labor Problems*, edited by J. R. Commons, 1905.

own. This was notably true during the crisis of 1893.[1] In the following table is summarized the total amount of benefits paid out, the sum paid under each form, and the relative importance of each benefit:[2]

TOTAL BENEFITS AND RELATIVE IMPORTANCE OF EACH FORM.
ANNUAL AVERAGE (1900–1905).

	Amount.	Per cent.
Sick benefit	$144,278	34
Death benefit	136,456	32
Strike benefit	65,316	15
Traveling loans	48,291	11
Out of employment	25,424	6
Total	419,765	100

Average cost per member $8.93.

It is noteworthy that the strike payments form a small percentage of the entire distribution of benefits, disproving the general belief that a union is merely a striking organization. The policy of strong unions, as with powerful nations, is one of armed peace. The Cigar Makers' Union is equipped with a fund approximating seven hundred thousand dollars.

The interesting as well as vital problem that presents itself, and which is causing no little apprehension among the union leaders, is, how long the union can maintain its position and influence in the face of two antagonistic forces, the trust and machinery. If, as seems not unlikely, efficient machinery should be introduced for the

[1] Those Unions that had strong benefit systems, like the Cigar Makers, Railroad Conductors, German American Typophria, suffered least. *Cf. Report of Ind. Com.*, vol. xvii, pp. 826, 280, 104. Whereas the Bricklayers', Plasterers', Woodcarvers' Unions, which had no such benefit system, suffered a great decline in union membership. *Cf. ibid.*, pp. 118, 154, 202.

[2] A very complete and detailed tabulation of these benefits for 26 years was published in the *Cigar Makers' Official Journal*, April 15th, 1906.

rolling and wrapping of cigars, as has been the case in the making of bunches, then the present supply of skilled labor will be supplanted by an unskilled grade of workers. This, of course, will affect only the manufacture of cheap scrap filler cigars, for no machine has yet been invented for the manufacture of long filler, high grade cigars. To the extent that machinery has been successfully introduced, women and children have taken the positions of skilled laborers, and the union has become to that extent actually, as well as potentially, weaker. The Union is offering stubborn resistance to the introduction of machinery, but its fight has been futile wherever the machine has been practical. In proportion as skill is made unnecessary, the union loses its hold on one of the means namely, its apprentice laws, whereby it controls the supply of labor. Moreover, the kind of laborers it must deal with—unskilled workers, women and children—becomes more difficult to organize.

Should fortune favor the Union, and no revolutionizing machinery be introduced, there would still be the Trust to cope with. The latter is rapidly extending its business in the cigar industry, and to that extent is depriving the Union of another weapon. At present the Union and the Trust are in open hostility, the Union taking sides with the independent manufacturers. So long as the Union can retain its hold over consumers—through the use of the Union label—it will be able to maintain its position against the Trust. But this is becoming daily more difficult, for with the organization of its United Cigar Stores the Trust is capturing a large portion of that retail trade which formerly went to small dealers whom the Union can more easily and effectively boycott than it can the Trust.

If both forces—machinery and the Trust—conquer,

the Union must inevitably lose some of its present power and prestige. Although machinery and the Trust are gaining ground, it is too early to venture a prediction concerning the ultimate outcome of the conflict. Should these anti-union forces win, the conditions in the cigar industry will become similar to those now prevailing in the manufacture of plug, chewing and smoking tobacco, snuff and cigarettes, conditions which, as we saw above, are so wretched that the status of the cigar makers to-day seems, by comparison, ideal.

Before concluding this chapter we wish to call attention briefly to the conditions in a specialized branch of the industry, the stogie trade. There are employed in Pittsburg and Wheeling, West Virginia, about ten thousand of these workers, some of whom are machine operators and receive low wages. A large proportion of stogies, however, are made by hand, like ordinary scrap or filler cigars. The hand-workers earn about five hundred dollars per year, which in general approximates the wage of the cigar makers. Because of trade disputes with respect to the wage scale, attitude towards machinery and minimum selling-price to jobbers and retailers the stogie makers are not affiliated with the Cigar Makers' Union, but have an independent organization known as the National Stogie Makers' League,[1] with a present membership of one thousand, or about ten per cent of the entire number of workers.

Our wonderful economic prosperity seems not to have improved the conditions of the laborers in the tobacco industry. Where machinery has displaced skilled by unskilled labor, as in the manufacture of plug, smoking

[1] It was organized in 1896 by its present president, W. H. Riley. The Union's headquarters are at Wheeling, W. Va.

and chewing tobacco, machine cigarettes and machine cigars and stogies, the hours of labor are from nine to ten hours per day, and the yearly income averages but three hundred dollars. Where much skill is still required, as in the manufacture of mold and hand-made cigars, the workers, with the aid of an efficient organization, earn from five hundred to six hundred dollars per year. Even for the more favorably situated laborers, therefore, wages are not far above the level of bare subsistence.

CHAPTER VI

Foreign Trade

SECTION I. EXPORTS

For almost three centuries we have been not only the largest producer, but also the leading exporter of tobacco in the world. Except during periods of temporary disturbance our cultivation and exportation of leaf tobacco have kept pace with the general increase in consumption. Of our entire crop (approximately 700,000,000 pounds) nearly one-half is destined annually for European markets. It is only in the production of the highest grade of cigar leaf, supplied by Cuba and Sumatra, that we are unable to compete in the world market. The entire international trade in unmanufactured tobacco exceeds 600,000,000 pounds, and of this over fifty per cent is exported by the United States.[1]

It is no mere accident that we have been able to retain our supremacy in the tobacco market, for the extent and natural fertility of our lands have enabled us to produce the leaf used in ordinary consumption at a lower cost than is possible in other countries. Crops of inferior quality are grown and exported by Brazil, Hungary, India and the Dutch East Indies, but only to the extent of 100,000,000 pounds. Were it not for the high tariffs that protect the leaf grown in Russia, Hungary and Germany, practically the entire European market for leaf

[1] *Cf. Yearbook of the U. S. Department of Agriculture*, 1905, p. 715.

used in the manufacture of plug, chewing tobacco, pipe smoking tobacco, snuff and cigarettes, and a medium grade of cigar leaf would be supplied by our farmers.

The peculiar phenomenon in the leaf market is the element of monopoly enjoyed by producers whose leaf has once won popular favor among the consumers. Since there is no absolute objective standard for measuring the respective merits of leaf tobacco, it is difficult for the producers of a new leaf to dislodge the competitor already in control of the market. The cultivated taste and traditional preference of European consumers for American leaf have to that extent conferred upon our producers a semi-monopoly advantage. The American farmer is striving now to overcome the traditional bias of the American public for Sumatra wrapper leaf, just as Porto Rico is attempting, not as yet with very much success, to persuade us that the quality of her cigar leaf is equal to that grown in Cuba. This lack of standardization and of uniformity in quality, is one of the peculiarities of the tobacco leaf market.

To appreciate the conditions and problems in the foreign markets, we must bear in mind two factors. First, most governments still continue to view tobacco as a source of revenue. This explains the unusually high tariff duty on tobacco in European countries, which, while it puts us on an equal footing with foreign producers, gives the farmers of those particular high-tariff countries an advantage over our own. Secondly, the governments of several large European countries—France, Austria, Spain, Italy—exercise a monopoly over the sale of tobacco. These "Régie" countries make all their purchases of leaf through government agents, who can buy from domestic or foreign producers. The government's revenue consists in the net surplus of the selling price over the purchasing price. The disadvantage of this system—to the producers—arises not only from the tendency to fix the selling price as high as possible, thus diminishing consumption and the demand for the finished product, but also from the fact that all competition for raw material is eliminated on the side of the buyers.

Whether burdened directly by import duties, or indirectly through the "Régie," the tax on tobacco is exceedingly high. England's minimum duty on imported tobacco is seventy-seven cents per pound which in the case of American leaf, marketing at ten cents, is equivalent to a seven hundred per cent *ad valorem* duty.[1] Germany's tariff on tobacco is eighty-five marks per one hundred kilograms, or about eight cents per pound, which is equivalent to a one hundred per cent *ad valorem* duty on our leaf.[2] In "Régie" countries the tax on our leaf, which wholesales at eight cents per pound, is as follows: in Italy ninety-one cents per pound, in France eighty cents, in Austria thirty-five cents and in Hungary thirty cents per pound. The price of leaf tobacco in these countries is fixed arbitrarily by the government.

With this general character of the foreign market in mind, let us measure our foreign leaf trade statistically. Our exports, since the Civil War, have more than doubled in quantity: in the ten year period prior to 1860 they were annually 145,000,000 pounds whereas from 1895 to 1905 the figures exceeded 313,000,000 pounds annually.[3]

[1] England's import duty is 77 cents per pound on tobacco containing more than 10 per cent. moisture, otherwise 85 cents per pound.

[2] Under the new law which went into effect July 1, 1906, the import duty on cigarettes and cigarette leaf tobacco is 76 cents per pound.

[3] Based on statistics of *Yearbook of U. S. Department of Agriculture* and *Annual Reports of Commerce and Navigation*.

As our total annual production in the last decade averaged 660,000,000 pounds, our exports were approximately forty-seven per cent of our entire crop, and were valued roughly at twenty-five million dollars annually. In the following table is represented the distribution of our exports, and their proportion of the entire tobacco trade of those several European countries which are the largest importers of our leaf: [1]

FOREIGN TOBACCO TRADE OF THE UNITED STATES.

Name of Country.	Percentage of the total United States crop exported (quantity).	Percentage of total importation imported from United States (quantity).
England	31	83
Germany	16	17 [2]
France	10	65
Italy	10	90
Netherlands	6	50
Spain	5	40

Of the total quantity consumed (600,000,000 pounds) in these six countries, over fifty per cent is American tobacco, about twenty-five per cent is home-grown, and the remainder is imported from the Dutch East Indies, Brazil, Cuba and the Philippine Islands. Russia and Hungary are the only countries which produce for exportation as well as for their own consumption, and consequently our trade with these nations is nil. Japan also produces her own leaf tobacco, under a governmental monopoly. Canada, on the other hand, imports almost her total supply of 10,000,000 pounds annually from the United States.

[1] In this table the percentage of our crop exported is a ten-year average; the percentage of foreign imports is a five-year average.

[2] Germany imports thirty-five per cent of her tobacco from the East India islands, twenty per cent from Brazil, and nine per cent from Cuba.

Our export leaf, which is destined almost exclusively for the manufacture of plug, chewing and smoking tobacco, snuff and cigarettes, is largely confined to two general types. One is the "Heavy Shipping" tobacco, grown along the Mississippi River, in western Kentucky and Tennessee and in the famous Clarksville region which lies between the Cumberland and Tennessee rivers. The second type is the Burley leaf, raised chiefly in central and northern Kentucky and in several counties in Kentucky and Ohio bordering on the Ohio River. It is grown to some extent in Maryland, Missouri and Illinois. Virginia's shipping crop comprises both the Heavy Shipping and Burley leaf besides some superior wrapper leaf. North Carolina produces the cigarette filler and plug wrapper. The Burley leaf is the better of the two types, and is shipped most heavily to Great Britain, the lower grades going to continental countries. None of our genuine cigar leaf is exported, although Italy and Spain use these cheaper Southern leaves in the manufacture of cigars and cheroots.

As domestic manufacturers and foreign buyers purchase an equal amount of our leaf, prices are fixed, theoretically, by a combination of both demands, domestic and foreign. In fact, however, prices have been, to some extent, arbitrarily regulated by the Trust in agreement with the "Régie" agents, both together using about seventy per cent of the entire crop. As a rule, domestic manufacturers use the higher grade of leaf, and foreign buyers, with the exception of Great Britain take a lower grade. When prices rise, either through a greater demand at home or a shortage in the crop, foreign buyers substitute a lower grade of leaf for the one they have been previously using. This circumstance makes it very difficult to study the relation of prices and foreign shipments. Prices of export leaf since 1875 have remained very steady, as shown in the following table:

EXPORTATION OF UNMANUFACTURED TOBACCO—QUANTITY, VALUE AND PRICE. (1860–1905.)

Annual Average.	Total Quantity.	Total Value.	Price per Pound.
1859–1861	175,000,000 lbs.	$16,000,000	9.2 cents.
1862–1865	110,000,000	19,000,000	18.0 "
1866–1870	190,000,000	22,723,000	11.9 "
1871–1875	240,000,000	24,474,000	10.1 "
1876–1880	264,000,000	23,560,000	8.9 "
1881–1885	225,000,000	19,400,000	8.4 "
1886–1890	268,000,000	23,084,000	8.8 "
1891–1895	272,000,000	22,895,090	8.8 "
1896–1900	300,000,000	25,268,000	8.6 "
1901–1905	325,000,000	29,558,000	8.6 "

Since 1860 our exports have increased eighty-five per cent in quantity and eighty per cent in value, which, at the present time, comprises about three per cent of our total agricultural export trade. Our leading internal markets for the sale of this tobacco leaf are Louisville, Cincinnati, Clarksville (Tennessee), Hopkinsville and Paducah. From these tobacco centers most of the leaf is sent by rail to New York, Baltimore and New Orleans; these three ports ship abroad ninety per cent of our leaf exports. The freight rates from these inland markets to the shipping ports average about thirty cents per one hundred pounds, which is equivalent to a three per cent *ad valorem* transportation rate.

Though steadily increasing, our exportation of manufactured products is still slight as compared with our leaf exports. To begin with, the markets of France, Italy, Spain and other "Régie" countries, including Japan, are closed to us, since the governments in these countries exercise a monopoly over the manufacture and sale of tobacco products: England's market is largely non-competitive, as the result of an agreement with English manufacturers,[1] whereby the Trust is not to compete in Great Britain. Germany is closed to us because of her high tariff rates: thirty cents per pound on manufactured goods and only nine cents on raw leaf.[2] In countries that do not discriminate against our manufactured products we can not compete because of the difference in the cost of labor, especially in cigars, where hand labor is so essential. In the manufacture of products other than cigars, in which machinery is more important than labor, we enjoy no technical advantages sufficient to offset the difference in general labor costs and foreign tariff duties. Consequently our exports to Europe are very insignificant, amounting all told, in 1905, to $635,000, which comprises only eleven per cent of our total exports of manufactured tobacco products, and of this one-half is shipped to the United Kingdom, partly for transshipment. Our largest foreign markets are Asia and Oceanica, as shown in the following table:[3]

SUMMARY OF FOREIGN TRADE IN MANUFACTURED TOBACCO: ANNUAL AVERAGE 1900–1904.

	Plug.	Cigarettes.	Chewing and Smoking Tobacco, Snuff.	Cigars
Total	$2,240,000	$2,200,000	$930,000	$49,000
Asia	1 %	54 %	14 %	4 %
Chinese Empire.				
British India.				
Oceanica	41 %	19 %	30 %	28 %
B. Australia, etc.				
Europe	33 %	16 %	30 %	14 %
United Kingdom.				
Germany.				
Africa	1 %	10 %	1 %	1 %
North America	12 %	1 %	17 %	32 %
Canada.				
West Indies.				

[1] *Supra*, p. 114. [2] *Supra*, p. 168, note 2.

[3] *Cf. Commerce and Navigation of the U. S., Annual Report Treasury Dept.*, 1904, vol. ii, pp. 728 *et seq.*

Our tobacco manufacturers, especially the Trust, are energetically developing the markets in the Orient and Australia.[1] It is this extension of trade in these non-European regions that is responsible for the steady and constant increase in our recent export trade. The three million dollar mark of 1860 was not exceeded until 1890 ($3,876,045); since 1890 the trade has grown to $5,-690,203 in 1905. Our combined export trade of leaf and manufactured products reached $35,000,000 in 1905.

Summarizing the account of our export tobacco trade, we supply Europe with one-half or more of the entire amount of leaf used in the manufacture of plug, chewing and smoking tobacco, snuff and cigarettes; but our growers have no natural monopoly, for besides producing large quantities, Europe can substitute leaf from Java, Brazil and the Philippines. In the production of the higher grades of cigarette and cigar leaf, we can not compete with Turkey and Algeria, in the former, and with Cuba and Sumatra, in the latter. For a combination of reasons,—the existence of government ("Régie") monopolies in European countries, discriminating tariff duties, the Trust's agreement not to market its goods in Great Britain, and the difference in the wages of labor,—our finished products have thus far found very little sale in European countries. The chief markets for our manufactures, principally cigarettes and plug, are respectively Asia (Chinese Empire and British India) and Oceanica (Australia).

[1] Just as soon as the Japanese government had declared Dalny (Manchuria) an open port, the British-American Tobacco Company, controlled by the American Trust, was on the spot offering tobacco products at greatly reduced rates, in competition with the Japanese goods.

SECTION II. IMPORTS AND THE TARIFF.

In as much as we export not only the raw material, but also the finished products of manufactured tobacco, (plug, smoking and chewing tobacco, snuff and cigarettes), it is obvious that our problems with respect to our import trade must be confined almost exclusively to cigar leaf and cigars. It is our purpose, in this section, to measure the real significance of our import trade, and to observe how our domestic growers and manufacturers have faced the problems arising therefrom.

Our leaf tobacco imports, prior to 1846, were too insignificant to merit our attention. In the decade, however, from 1850 to 1860, coincident with the expansion of our home market for cigars, our importation of leaf sprang into prominence. In the five year period, prior to the Civil War, it amounted annually to $1,184,916, imported principally from Cuba. The import movement in manufactured products (plug, chewing and smoking tobacco and snuff) was even more insignificant, for in the entire period, from 1790 to 1860, the imports were less than three-quarters of a million dollars, comprising chiefly a fine grade of snuff and smoking tobacco imported from England. Cigars alone occupied a prominent place among our imports, reaching in 1836 one million dollars annually, in 1851 two million dollars, and finally, in 1860 $4,586,742. These cigars were imported from Germany and Cuba, the very cheap grade from the former, and the highest grade from the latter country. The largest portion came from Germany, where they were made by very cheap labor under the household system of production. In 1860 the value of our imports was distributed as follows:

TOBACCO IMPORTS IN 1860.

	Value.	Per cent.
Total	$6,077,901	100
Cigars	4,581,551	75.3
Unmanufactured leaf	1,365,625	22.4
Manufactured tobacco	132,725	2.3

With the introduction of a high war tariff in 1862 came a sudden and permanent diminution in the importation of cigars. In July of 1862 the duty was increased from twenty cents to thirty-five cents per pound, or from two dollars to three dollars and a half per thousand cigars, which were valued, when imported, at only six dollars per thousand. This was an advance of nearly one hundred per cent in the *ad valorem* duty. The tariff was further increased during the war, finally reaching, in 1866 to 1868, three dollars per pound in addition to a fifty per cent *ad valorem* duty. From 1867 to 1890 it remained unchanged, a combination of a specific duty, at two dollars and fifty cents per pound, and an *ad valorem* duty of twenty-five per cent. The McKinley Tariff of 1890 raised it still higher to four dollars and fifty cents per pound, plus the twenty-five per cent *ad valorem* duty, which, except for the temporary reduction under the Wilson Act of 1894, and a special reduction of twenty per cent on Cuban goods,[1] has remained intact to the present day.

Concretely what this tariff has meant is this: that from 1867 to 1890 (at $2.50 per pound plus twenty-five per cent *ad valorem*) a duty of at least five cents was levied on each cigar imported, and from 1890 to the present time ($4.50 per pound plus twenty-five per cent

[1] By the terms of the reciprocity treaty of 1902 between the U. S. and Cuba, the latter's products are admitted into our country at a 20 per cent reduction of the rate provided for under the Dingley tariff.

ad valorem less twenty per cent on Cuban goods) each cigar imported has been burdened with a tax of at least six cents. The consequence has been that only the finest and highest priced cigars can be imported. The tariff to-day is equivalent to a one hundred per cent *ad valorem* duty on all but the most expensive cigars, which is ample protection to home manufacturers of cigars of the cheaper grades. Our manufacturers sell to retailers clear Havana cigars, which retail at ten cents, for sixty dollars per thousand, whereas the minimum tariff is at least that amount.

A comparison of the quantity and value of cigars imported, prior and subsequent to these high tariff schedules, will indicate what the effect has been. This can best be seen in a table like the following:

IMPORTATION OF CIGARS.[1]

Annual Average.	Quantity.	Value.
1855–1859	8,000,000 lbs.	$4,021,300
1865–1869	667,380	1,479,000
1875–1879	658,000	2,399,459
1885–1889	1,000,000	3,329,186
1895–1899	418,000	1,984,099
1900–1904	515,000	2,687,307

Taking the entire period, the decline in quantity has been about ninety-two per cent, and in value only fifty per cent. Prior to the war our imported cigars constituted over fifty per cent of the entire home consumption, whereas they to-day form less than one-half of one per cent. It should be observed that the decline in imports was very heavy subsequent to the sudden and large increase in the tariff of 1890, the rate advancing from one hundred to one hundred and twenty per cent *ad valorem*.

[1] *Cf.* "Statistics of Manufactures of Tobacco," in *Tenth Census of U. S.*, p. 48.

With the twenty per cent reduction in the duty, as a result of the Cuban reciprocity of 1902, our imports rose appreciably. In the three-year period, from 1900 to 1902 (inclusive) we received eighteen per cent of Cuba's total cigar exports, whereas from 1903 to 1905 (inclusive) we took twenty-five per cent. Of her total cigar output, Cuba sends to England forty per cent, compared with twenty-five per cent to the United States, thirteen per cent to Germany and four per cent to France. Practically all our cigar imports come from Cuba.

During the development and expansion of the cigar industry, our producers of raw material were likewise taking advantage of the high tariff, which originated in, and continued in operation since, the Civil War. In 1862 the duty was raised from twenty-five per cent *ad valorem* to thirty-five cents per pound, which was equivalent to seventy-five per cent *ad valorem*. As our ordinary cigar domestic filler leaf sells to the manufacturer for about twelve to fifteen cents per pound, this tariff practically excluded all but the finest Cuban filler, just as the tariff on cigars had operated to keep out all but the most expensive grades of cigars. Consequently the production of filler leaf was greatly stimulated in Connecticut, Ohio, Pennsylvania and New York. These growers, who have enjoyed undisturbed protection since 1862[1] are beginning to show some anxiety over the proposed reduction of the tariff on Philippine cigar leaf, which would compete with their own products, especially cigar fillers and binders.[2]

[1] By the Cuban reciprocity treaty of 1902, a 20 per cent reduction is allowed on Cuban leaf, making the duty 28 cents instead of 35 cents per pound.

[2] The Payne Bill, which passed the House and is now in the hands of the Ways and Means Committee of the Senate, provides for a 75 per cent reduction of the tariff rate under the Dingley Act.

They have reasons to feel worried, for the present output of this Philippine leaf is over twenty million pounds, or fifteen per cent of our entire cigar leaf crop, and it can be produced at five cents per pound, or about two cents per pound lower than our own leaf. With an improvement in the methods of cultivation, and an extension of its production, this leaf, which is now shipped to Spain and Austria-Hungary, may easily become, under a lower tariff, a competitor of our domestic product.

The high tariff has not, however, been able to exclude the Cuban cigar filler, which is universally regarded as superior in quality to any grown in the world. All efforts to transplant it to our soil, or even to produce a fair substitute, have thus far been fruitless. While our domestic grown filler of Connecticut, Ohio and New York has doubtless been improved as a result of these efforts, it is still used almost exclusively in five-cent cigars; whereas, the Cuban filler is destined, invariably, only for the higher priced cigars. After much experimentation, and only with the aid of a higher protective tariff, Florida filler may be said to be the sole direct competitor of the Cuban leaf. The semi-monopoly, which the latter enjoys in the market, is due to a combination of a peculiar soil and a favorable climate. Besides these natural advantages, its production requires a large amount of skilled human industry. Its cost of cultivation is averaged at forty cents per pound, and it has been marketed, in a twenty year period, at forty-eight cents per pound. Cultivation in Cuba is largely confined to three western provinces, Pinar del Rio (70 per cent), Habana (13 per cent), Santa Clara (13 per cent). In the first is located the most famous tobacco district of Cuba, the Vuelto Abajo.

Though our import movement of Cuban leaf may have

been retarded, it has not suffered any diminution under the operation of our high tariff since the Civil War, as indicated in the following table:

IMPORTATION OF CUBAN FILLER—1855-1905.

Annual Average for Five Year Period.	Pounds.	Per cent of Domestic Cigars Made of Cuban Filler.
1855-1860	7,014,485	Uncertain [1]
1861-1865	5,666,464	Uncertain [2]
1866-1870	4,116,595	13
1871-1875	8,985,465	21
1876-1880	7,255,663	14
1881-1885	11,536,374	20
1886-1890	15,532,975	27
1891-1895	15,344,466	23
1896-1900	10,811,173 [3]	14 [3]
1901-1905	24,048,837	24

These figures show an increase of sixty-six per cent in the quantity of leaf imported since 1855-1860. This offsets the large diminution in imported Cuban cigars in the same period. Clearly what has happened is this, the Cuban cigar industry has, to a very large extent, been transferred to the United States. Instead of importing the finished product, we have encouraged the importation of the raw material and have caused the cigars to be manufactured here. In the period from 1900 to 1905, we purchased over seventy per cent of Cuba's total crop. And our proportion is gradually increasing both in quantity and in value. In 1900 we received only fifty-six per

[1] There are no reliable statistics of domestic production for this period.

[2] Owing to the great amount of cigars that escaped the revenue inspector during the Civil War, it is impossible to estimate our domestic production.

[3] Cultivation in Cuba was checked by the disturbances of the Spanish-Cuban-American War.

cent and in 1904–1905 seventy-seven per cent of her entire supply. The value of these imports has advanced from $8,478,251 in 1900, to $13,348,000 in 1905.

Florida has profited most by this movement of part of the Cuban cigar industry to our country. Tampa and Key West have taken away from Cuba not only the raw material, but also many of the skilled laborers. In the twenty-year period, from 1886 to 1906, Florida's output of cigars increased from 92,000,000 to 331,000,000, an advance of two hundred and sixty per cent. The capital invested in the cigar factories, reported by the United States Census, rose from $1,686,396 in 1890, to $5,349,-907 in 1900 and $7,383,963 in 1905. The product increased in value from eight to sixteen million dollars. In fact, Florida alone manufactures fifty per cent more Havana cigars than are made in Cuba. The latter's output is about two hundred million, whereas, the former's is over three hundred million cigars. About seventy-five per cent of the leaf grown in Cuba is consumed in the United States.

A second problem with respect to the importation of leaf tobacco is concerned with the substitution of the foreign-grown Sumatra leaf for our domestic cigar wrapper. This silky, elastic, yellow-spotted, Sumatra cigar wrapper has grown in popularity since its introduction into this country in the seventies. It was to check its importation that an alteration in the tariff schedules in 1883 was made, whereby the general duty of thirty-five cents per pound was retained for filler and a seventy-five cent duty was levied on all wrapper leaf. The McKinley Tariff increased the rate to two dollars per pound, but the Dingley schedule put it at one dollar and eighty-five cents per pound, which, except for the twenty per cent reduction allowed on Cuban wrappers, is still in operation to-day. As Sumatra sells at the general market, Amsterdam and Hamburg, for fifty cents per pound, the present tax is equivalent to a three hundred per cent *ad valorem* duty, causing the price in our home market to range from three dollars per pound upwards. In spite, however, of this extraordinarily high tariff, we have continued to increase our consumption of this wrapper leaf. The following table presents both the quantity imported and the relative proportion of cigars wrapped with this leaf:

IMPORTATION AND CONSUMPTION OF SUMATRA LEAF—1880–1905.

Annual Average.	Sumatra Leaf Imported. Lbs.	Cigars Wrapped with Imported Sumatra.	Total Production of Domestic Cigars.	Per cent of Sumatra Cigars of Total Production in U. S.
1881–1885	194,857	34,951,000	3,153,215,366	01
1886–1890	1,123,214	374,404,000	3,819,841,450	10
1891–1895	3,381,000	1,127,000,000	4,413,755,834	25
1896–1900	4,789,606	1,566,535,000	4,850,464,121	32
1901–1905	6,431,392	2,143,794,000	6,649,390,864	32

From which figures it appears that our consumers are increasingly preferring this Sumatra on their cigars. The total value of our imported wrapper leaf from 1896 to 1900 has averaged annually over five million dollars. It is not at all unlikely that if it were not burdened with so high a tariff duty it would completely supplant our two domestic competitors, the Connecticut seed wrapper and the Florida imitation-Sumatra wrapper. Although our seed wrapper costs the manufacturer only from forty-five to sixty cents per pound, and the Sumatra leaf from eighty to ninety cents per pound in bond (in American markets), the former affords a poorer return; whereas six pounds of seed wrapper are required for covering one thousand cigars, only three pounds, or less, of Sumatra are needed. Under free trade, or only a light tariff duty, the two would stand on the same footing so far as relative costs to the manufacturer are concerned. The Florida wrapper, which is inferior in quality to the genuine Sumatra, sells for about two dollars per pound, and could never compete with the latter except under a very high protective tariff. We have, by our tariff, encouraged the production in Florida of leaf under extremely costly processes. Realizing the value of this Sumatra leaf, our United States Department of Agriculture has been carrying on experiments for ten years, with the view of raising this leaf on our soil (in Connecticut, Georgia, Florida) but its efforts, thus far, have been futile.

In the sale of their tobacco, the growers of Sumatra, like the producers of Cuban leaf, enjoy a semi-monopoly to the extent that they possess the peculiarly favorable soil, in the supply of which nature seems to have been niggardly. Most of this choice and limited supply of tobacco land in the island of Sumatra is in the control of Dutch syndicates, the most famous of which is the "Deli Maatschappy," which produces about one-third of the total crop. This single company, with a capital stock of over a million and a half dollars, has been declaring one hundred per cent dividends annually for over twenty years.

The tariff problem in the tobacco industry is complicated by the traditional fiscal policy adopted with respect to it. There seems to prevail a tacit belief that a government ought to derive from this particular industry as much revenue as possible. Judged by this latter criterion, our own government is very successful, for in the nine-year period, from 1897 to 1905, it has derived annually, in the form of tariff duties on tobacco, no less than $17,500,000 on imported goods valued at $15,500,000, which made the tariff rate one hundred and thirteen per cent *ad valorem:* two and one-half million from cigars on a one hundred per cent duty five million from filler leaf on a seventy-five per cent duty, and ten million from wrappers on a two hundred per cent basis.

When distributed among the various elements and classes in the industry and among consumers, the burden occasioned by this high duty is borne without any complaint or great hardship. In the case of imported cigars, the consumers, by the very fact of their being able to purchase so expensive a grade of goods, are able to bear the incidence of the tax, which does undoubtedly fall upon them. The tax on Sumatra is, in effect, five dollars per thousand cigars, which is equivalent to a burden of one-half of one cent on each cigar consumed. The tax on Cuban filler is even less than this amount, approximately, four dollars per thousand, or four-tenths of one cent on each cigar. Because of the insignificance of the burden, a reduction in the tariff might not in the least redound to the benefit of the consumer, but in all likelihood, would confer a larger element of profit upon the retailer. Nor must it be forgotten, that the imported unmanufactured leaf is, in some respects, non-reproducible, since the cultivation can not easily be extended. A reduction of the tariff might conceivably, therefore, merely confer an added advantage upon these Cuban and Sumatra land owners. To the extent, however, that these producers enjoy only a partial monopoly, and that the cultivation of these import types could be further extended, even under increasing costs, the price of this leaf would be lower, and the consumer might then receive a slightly better quality of cigar than he is at present obtaining without any increase in price. With the duty on Sumatra and Cuban filler greatly reduced, our domestic manufacturer could always afford to use the former on five cent cigars. and some quantity of the latter. In our opinion, a reduction of the tariff would be followed, not by any single one of these alternatives, but by a combination of them. The revenues relinquished by the government would go, in part, to the consumer in the form of an improved quality of his cigar; partly to the retailer, since the latter would be able to buy cheaper from the manufacturers; and partly to foreign landowners, who would profit by an increase in the demand for their particular crops.

In conclusion, it ought to be said, that the interests of American farmers and manufacturers are not identical. The farmer has been clamoring for high duty on raw material—Cuban filler and Sumatra wrapper; whereas the manufacturer has been equally desirous of obtaining, not only high duties on manufactured products, but low rates on raw material. Our high tariffs on raw material and manufactured cigars have artificially stimulated the production of both; as, for instance, the Florida-Sumatra leaf and the transplanting of the Cuban cigar industry to Tampa and Key West. In both instances economic waste is involved. It is also worth noting, in conclusion, that over three hundred million pounds of exported leaf are valued at only twenty-five million dollars, compared with fifteen million dollars for thirty million pounds of imported leaf. This means that we export an inferior grade and import a superior grade of leaf.

CHAPTER VII

The Tobacco Tax

It is possible for a government to adopt one of at least four different attitudes or policies toward an industry: it may assume a purely negative or *laissez-faire* attitude; it may, for social reasons, supervise and regulate certain features of the industry, as when it attempts to regulate railroad rates; it may adopt a purely fiscal policy, in connection with which the industry is considered as a source of public revenue; or lastly, it may, for broad socio-economic reasons, assume the responsibility of directly owning and operating the entire industry, as in the case of government ownership of the post office or railroads. Although we shall have occasion, in passing, to compare the operation of these various policies with respect to the tobacco industry, our study will be confined largely to the fiscal relation between our own government and this industry. Our policy has not been unique, for all important countries have, for centuries, regarded the tobacco industry principally in the light of a revenue yielder.

Having adopted the fiscal attitude, it still remains to select that particular method of taxing the industry which will be most lucrative to the government and least injurious to the development of the industry itself. Which system this is to be will depend largely, but not altogether, upon the primary economic status of the industry with respect to each particular country. Nations that import most of their raw material—leaf tobacco—as do England, Germany, Belgium, Holland, Norway and Sweden, find the customs system as serviceable as any. Some importing countries, however, as for instance France, Austria, Spain, Italy and Portugal exercise a government monopoly over the purchase and sale of tobacco; in which instance, the public revenue is equivalent to the surplus of the selling price over the purchasing price or cost of production, and consists not merely of the tax paid ordinarily by the consumer, through an impost, but includes also that portion of the trade profits which formerly went to the manufacturer, jobber and retailer. It is obvious that countries producing largely for home consumption and exportation, can not rely on an import duty. They can, however, like Japan, exercise a complete monopoly or government "Régie" as it is called; or such countries like Russia, Germany and the United States may utilize as a supplement to an import duty, the excise or internal revenue system, whereby a tax is levied on all articles of consumption. While these various systems of taxation are not readily interchangeable, it frequently happens that alternative policies are presented to a single country. To reach the largest portion of tobacco consumed in our country, which is home grown, we employ an excise stamp tax: whereas, Japan, similarly situated, accomplishes the same end through a government monopoly over the entire industry.

Prior to the Civil War our internal revenue tax was resorted to only on two different occasions. In 1794 a tax was levied on manufactured tobacco to help defray the costs of administrating the national government. It gave rise to so much discontent, however, that it was abandoned after being in operation but two years.[1] It was again introduced during the War of 1812, but remained in effect only until 1816, when the national government returned to dependence for its revenues upon tariff duties. The excise tax was not attempted again until 1862, when the financial stress of the rebellion imposed upon the national government the utilization of all available sources of revenue.

Thrust upon the government so suddenly, with little time for public discussion and consideration, the excise system, adopted in July, 1862, was naturally crude and unsatisfactory in many respects.[2] At first, the proposal was made to tax the raw material as well as the finished product. But it was considered either impossible or too costly for the government agent to search out and tax the raw material, which was grown so extensively. Consequently the proposed tax on raw leaf was never embodied in the law. Moreover, the original excise measure provided for an *ad valorem*, as well as a specific tax on the finished product: goods valued above thirty cents per pound were taxed fifteen cents; for those under thirty cents the tax was ten cents per pound. As it was left to the manufacturer to assess his wares,[3] this system put a premium upon dishonesty. These abuses were remedied by abandoning, in 1863, the *ad valorem* feature in manufactured tobacco and in 1868 in cigars. A more

[1] The net revenue to the government during these two years was only $26,961.

[2] The act did not go into operation until September of 1862. For a detailed description of the various changes in the development of our internal revenue tobacco tax, *cf.* "The Tobacco Tax," by Frank L. Olmsted, *Quarterly Journal of Economics*, Jan., 1891.

[3] Government assessors were appointed in each district to assist the tax collector settle disputes arising from doubtful assessments or valuations.

serious weakness in the system was the absence of any method whereby the government revenue officials could detect violations of the law, since it was impossible to discriminate the untaxed from the taxed products. The tax was paid by the manufacturer after his products had left the factory and were beyond the reach of the inspector or tax collector. In 1863 a branding process was introduced, but this too was ineffective.[1] Finally, in 1868, came the method now in vogue, the use of a government adhesive stamp on all packages containing manufactured products. As a further check upon possible fraud, an inventory system was introduced requiring the manufacturer, as well as the leaf dealer, to report to the government a detailed monthly statement of the quantity of his purchases and sales. By 1870 this remodeled system had proved its efficiency.[2]

The principal features of the tax of 1870 have remained in operation to this day. There is no tax on raw material, as such, in the hands of either the farmer or the leaf jobber.[3] No tobacco, however, can be sold to the consumer without first bearing a government stamp. All finished products are taxable to the manufacturer.

[1] Inspectors were commissioned by the government to attach to each package of tobacco a seal or mark noting the quality and weight, etc., of said branded package. By collusion between the inspector and manufacturer the government was often defrauded of its proper revenues.

[2] The new features and amendments to the system adopted in 1868 were the outcome of a convention of tobacco and cigar manufacturers at Cleveland in 1867. Mr. D. A. Wells recommended many of the admirable features subsequently adopted by the convention and later embodied in the law of 1868. *Cf. Report of Special Commissioner of Internal Revenue*, 1868; also regular report of same year.

[3] There is now pending in Congress a bill which permits growers to sell leaf tobacco directly to the consumers without paying the tax which is at present required.

The latter being made responsible for the tax, he is required by law, as suggested above, to submit to the national government a detailed monthly and annual report of the quantity of leaf purchased and goods manufactured, so that the amount of government stamps purchased by him may tally with the amount of merchandise manufactured. For administrative purposes the country is divided into sixty-six revenue districts, in each of which is a collector of revenues, clerks and deputies. Final authority and responsibility are centralized in a commissioner of internal revenue, within the jurisdiction of the Treasury Department. And lastly the tax itself has remained specific; the rate at present, for instance, being three dollars per thousand cigars irrespective of their value; cigarettes one dollar and eight cents per thousand; manufactured tobacco and snuff are taxed, irrespective of their values, six cents per pound.[1]

Owing to the rapid increase in tobacco consumption since the Civil War, the government has found it possible to reduce the rate of taxation without occasioning any permanent diminution in the net revenue collected. As a result, however, of too sudden changes in the rate of the tax, sharp temporary fluctuations in the revenue were experienced. The relation between the rate of the tax and the net revenue with respect to manufactured tobacco is indicated in the following table:[2]

[1] Small cigars, however, weighing three pounds or less per thousand, are taxed only 54 cents per thousand. Likewise, cigarettes, weighing three pounds or less, are taxed 54 cents per thousand.

[2] For rates of tax and revenues collected from 1863 to 1900, *Cf. Report of Commissioner of Internal Revenue*, 1901, pp. 421-427.

RATE OF TAX AND NET REVENUE COLLECTED ON MANUFACTURED TOBACCO SINCE 1863.

	Rate of Tax.		Net Revenue.	
	Cents per Pound.	Percentage of Variation.	Dollars.	Percentage of Variation.
1863–1865	14		6,000,000	
1866–1872	30	+114	19,000,000	+210
1873–1879	22	— 26	25,000,000	+ 31
1880–1883	15	— 33	23,000,000	— 8
1884–1891	8	— 50	16,400,000	— 30
1892–1897	6	— 25	16,000,000	— .2
1898–1901	12	+100	34,000,000	+113
1902–1906	6	— 50	22,600,000	— 33

From this table it appears, that from 1866 to 1872 and from 1898 to 1901, the net revenues increased even more than the rate of the tax. The excess of increase is due, in the first period, to the improved system of collecting the revenues, explained above, and in the second period, to the absolute increase in the consumption of tobacco. If the increased tax affected the rate of per capita consumption, it was not to a sufficient extent to offset the absolute increase due to the growth of population. In every instance when the rate of tax was decreased, the net revenues suffered a smaller diminution: and in one period (1873–1879) an absolute increase in the revenues accompanied a lowering in the rate of tax. Both phenomena are again to be explained by the absolute increase in consumption.

This was equally true in the case of cigars and cigarettes. A fifty per cent reduction in the tax on cigars in 1883 (from six to three dollars per thousand), was accompanied by only a thirty per cent reduction in net revenues. A twenty per cent increase in the tax (war revenue), in 1898, was followed by a thirty-five per cent increase in the net revenues. When the war tax was removed (in 1902) the revenues, instead of falling off, actually increased over five per cent.[1] When the cigarette tax was reduced, in 1883, from one dollar and seventy-five cents to fifty cents per thousand (seventy per cent reduction), the net revenues fell off only thirty-eight per cent. When, however, the war revenue of 1898 increased the tax from fifty cents to one dollar and fifty cents per thousand, the net revenues advanced only twenty per cent. It appears that where the tax is already high, as on cigarettes, a further increase in the rate checks consumption. We present in the following table a summary of the net revenues to the government from the excise tax on tobacco in all its forms:

INTERNAL TOBACCO REVENUE.

Period.	Sum Collected Annually.	Remarks.
1863–1868	$13,019,000	High tax, but inefficient administrative system.
1869–1878	$35,000,000	High tax, but efficient system of collection and increased consumption of tobacco.
1879–1888	$35,000,000	Fifty per cent reduction in tax, accompanied however by increased consumption.
1889–1898	$32,000,000	Further reduction in tobacco tax. Consumption not heavy enough to offset reduction in tax.
1899–1901	$55,000,000	War occasioned great temporary increase in tax.
1902–1906	$45,000,000	War tax reduced on all tobacco but cigarettes,—consumption greatly increased.

Of our entire internal revenue from 1863 to 1906, collections from tobacco have comprised about twenty per

[1] *Cf. Report of Commissioner of Internal Revenue, 1901*, pp. 425–427. The revenue from 1880 to 1882 was $17,000,000, and from 1883 to 1885 $12,000,000 annually. From 1890 to 1901 it reached $19,000,000, and from 1902 to 1906, in spite of the tax reduction, $20,000,000.

cent; a little less than eighty per cent is derived from the tax on spirits and liquor.[1] Of the total tobacco revenue collected from 1902 to 1906, fifty per cent was derived from manufactured tobacco (plug, chewing and smoking tobacco and snuff), forty-five per cent from cigars and five per cent from cigarettes.[2] If to these internal revenue receipts we add the custom duties on tobacco ($21,500,000), the total income to the government, from 1902 to 1906, from its taxation of tobacco was $66,000,000 annually, which is about thirteen per cent of the national public revenues from all sources.

One of the fiscal merits of the internal revenue system is its flexibility. It can be made to yield a larger income without any serious disturbance to the industry. An instance of this occurred during the Spanish-American War, when the tax rate was increased one hundred per cent on manufactured tobacco, fifty per cent on cigarettes and twenty per cent on cigars, netting an increase of over seventy per cent in the total revenues, without causing the least friction or cessation of business at any point in the industry. The principal reason for this is due to the fact that, as the consumer is not asked to contribute directly through an increase in the price of his products, he is not likely to curtail his consumption. In the instance cited, instead of increasing the conventional price per unit, the manufacturer reduced slightly the quantity offered (*e. g.*, the ordinary three-ounce package smoking tobacco was reduced to two and one-

[1] The total internal revenue, annually (1903 to 1905), amounted to $232,000,000, of which $44,000,000 was derived from tobacco and $185,000,000 from spirits and liquor.

[2] $22,600,000 from manufactured tobacco, $20,000,000 from cigars, $2,600,000 from cigarettes.

half ounces) and a slightly inferior grade of leaf was substituted in the manufacture of cigars and cigarettes. Such a change is too insignificant to affect appreciably the rate of consumption. Consequently by a slight variation in the rate of the tax the revenues can be greatly increased or diminished without occasioning any serious disturbance within the industry.

To understand the effect and incidence of the tax, it is first necessary to study concretely the relation between the tax and the cost of production and price. Since the tax is specific and the cost of production varies with the quality of goods, it is impossible to state in general terms, for the entire trade, what proportion of the total cost the tax represents. On goods that retail for five cents per unit (*e. g.*, package of smoking tobacco or a single cigar) the tax comprises from fifteen to twenty-five per cent of the total cost of production. For instance, a fine five-cent cigar can be manufactured for twenty dollars per thousand, while the tax is three dollars a thousand, or fifteen per cent *ad valorem.* The ratio of the tax varies inversely with the quality and cost of goods. This is one of the defects of the present system, that a twenty-five-cent cigar pays no greater tax than a five-cent cigar. The tax on manufactured tobacco, like that on cigars, is six cents per pound, irrespective of the value of the finished products; while the tax on cigarettes is highest of all, thirty-eight cents per pound (one dollar and eight cents per thousand cigarettes weighing three pounds). On every five-cent package of chewing or smoking tobacco, snuff or cigarettes the consumer contributes to the government one cent, and on each cigar three-tenths of one cent. From the consumer's standpoint, therefore, it is equivalent to a consumption tax of at least twenty per cent on cigarettes, fifteen per cent on smoking and chewing tobacco, and six per cent on cigars.

Unconsciously, and therefore without complaint, the consumer is making this heavy contribution for the support of the national government; for as this tax enters as one of the fixed charges in the cost of production to the manufacturer in enters into price. The tax on manufactured tobacco (six cents per pound) exceeds the labor charges in the manufacture of the same; and in the manufacture of cigars, where hand labor is an important factor in production, the tax (three dollars per thousand, in addition to the import tax on cigar leaf, Sumatra and Cuban filler) is about fifty per cent of the labor costs; in cigarettes (at one dollar and eight cents per thousand or thirty-six cents per pound) the tax is equivalent to the cost of raw material and the wages combined. In the event of a sudden increase in the rate, the reason the consumer does not feel that the tax is shifted to him is due, as suggested above, to the fact that it takes the form of an alteration not in price, but in quality and quantity, and that the alteration is often either too subtle or too slight to make itself immediately felt.

That such a change in quality and quantity can be easily resorted to without materially checking consumption, is an indication that the industry is not taxed to its utmost. When we compare our tax with that of foreign countries, we realize how comparatively light our own is. This is brought out very clearly in the following table, which shows the relation between the rate of tax, the per capita consumption, the per capita tax and the total revenue:

RELATION BETWEEN THE RATE OF TAXATION, CONSUMPTION AND TOTAL REVENUES FROM TOBACCO.[1]

	Tax per Pound.	Per Capita Tax.	Per Capita Consumption.	Total Revenues.
France	76c.	$2.08	2.2 lbs.	$70,000,000
United States.....	15	.80	5.3	65,800,000
United Kingdom..	76	1.49	1.9	63,800,000
Italy	91	.95	1.0	31,000,000
Austria	35	1.64	3.0	27,000,000
Russia...........	16	.18	1.2	24,000,000
Germany.........	8	.28	3.5	16,500,000
Japan	16	.34	2.0	16,250,000
Hungary.........	29	.72	2.4	14,260,000
Belgium	3	.38	5.7	1,687,000

Where the tax is very high, as in Italy, France, the United Kingdom, Austria and Hungary, the tobacco revenue is contributed by fewer consumers than where the rate of the tax per pound is low as in our country, in Germany, Russia, Japan and Belgium. In the first group the tax is high enough to diminish both the number of consumers as well as the consumption per capita. In our own country consumption is heavy extensively as well as intensively. What we lose in revenues through the relatively low rate of tax, we gain by stimulating consumption among a greater number, as well as increasing the per capita consumption. Which, from a social point of view, is preferable, will depend on our attitude toward the question of the social utility of tobacco consumption. If we consider it a legitimate form of pleasure, then it is wiser to have a low tax, since the

[1] In this table the tax per pound refers to the duty and excise on each pound of leaf tobacco; the per capita tax is estimated on the basis of the entire population of the particular country; the per capita consumption is likewise based an the total population, not merely on the consumers of tobacco; the total revenues include both the customs duties and the excise tax wherever both exist, as in our own country.

poorer classes can thereby participate in the indulgence in a higher quality of tobacco at a moderate price. In France and England only the wealthy classes can afford to consume the higher grades of cigars and smoking tobacco.

The most equitable system would be an *ad valorem* tax, graduated so as to make the consumer contribute in direct proportion to the price of the commodity.[1] Our present excise system has no provision for an *ad valorem* rate, because as was discovered during the Civil War it is almost impossible to ascertain the true value of the finished products. Where we do attempt to apply the *ad valorem* tax, as in our import duty on leaf tobacco, it is inefficient. The duty calls for thirty-five cents per pound tax on fillers and one dollar and eighty-five cents per pound on wrappers. As a matter of fact, nearly all the leaf imported from Cuba, much of which is wrappers, enters under the thirty-five cent rate, (less twenty per reduction according to the reciprocity treaty of 1902). Although there are each year about four hundred million clear Havana cigars manufactured in this country, requiring (at the rate of four pounds of wrapper per one thousand cigars) a total of 1,600,000 pounds of wrappers, our government collects annually duty on less than seventy thousand pounds of Cuban wrappers. Through its inability to apply the *ad valorem* test, which is based on a rate discrimination between fillers and wrappers,[2]

[1] Japan's revenue stamp tax from 1876 to 1894 was an *ad valorem* impost, equivalent to two-tenths of the selling price. Its abuses were so great that the government finally established a Leaf Tobacco Monopoly in 1894.

[2] To be classed as wrappers, a bale of tobacco must contain more than 15 per cent wrappers. Of the entire leaf imported annually from Cuba, 21,000,000 pounds (from 1902 to 1906, inclusive), only 70,000 pounds were annually classed as wrappers.

there is a net loss to the government annually of two million dollars.

The difficulties in the way of a vigorous and just application of the *ad valorem* tax, either in our internal revenue system, or in our import duties, are obviated by a government monopoly over the industry like that exercised by France or Japan. Moreover, in such cases, the government being the sole buyer of leaf and the single manufacturer within the country, all smuggling and internal revenue frauds are practically eliminated. Both France and Japan own and operate exclusively the tobacco factories in their respective countries, and all retailers are supplied with goods direct from the government, through the latter's agents. The price of leaf, as well as the finished product, is fixed arbitrarily by the government.

As a method of taxation, a government monopoly is said to carry with it possible dangers and disadvantages. Fiscal considerations are often apt to lead a government to exploit the particular industry to the detriment of the general consuming public. In France and Italy the rate of profits, or the tax, represents about eighty per cent of the gross selling price of the finished product, as compared with a fifteen to twenty per cent tax in our own country.[1] Where the rate of profits is so high, the consumers are compelled to pay unreasonably high prices for their tobacco. For there is no good reason why this particular industry should be thus singled out and exploited for government revenues.

It must, however, be borne in mind that the excessive

[1] In 1904 the gross receipts of the French Tobacco Régie were $86,000,000, of which $80,000,000 was net profits or revenue for the government. In 1904-1905 the gross income of the Italian Tobacco Régie was $35,000,000, of which $25,000,000 was net profits or revenue for the government.

rate of profits under a government monopoly is no condemnation of the system as such. The tax on tobacco in England through the operation of an import duty is much higher than the tax in Japan, under a government monopoly. This much, however, must be granted, that when the industry is a private enterprise, the government's unreasonable policies are likely to meet with resistance from the capitalistic interests engaged in the industry.

Furthermore, it has been charged that the consumers suffer under a government monopoly as a result of the government's inefficiency as a producer. There is, however, no evidence to show that such is the case. The inferior quality of finished products offered to consumers in European countries may be due not to the particular methods of production, but rather to the conscious desire on the part of the government to increase its revenues by using, purposely, a less expensive grade of raw material.

Summarizing our discussion, therefore, we may say that the administrative features of our internal revenue stamp tax are fairly efficient but less so than under the operation of a government monopoly. For the latter, by exercising complete control over the entire industry, can prevent all smuggling and frauds. Moreover the "Régie" has the advantage of being able to apply successfully, as our system cannot, an *ad valorem* tax, since the government monopoly fixes the values and prices of all goods. While both systems of taxation are flexible, the "Régie" possesses the added merit of preventing an evasion of the increased tax when a change is made in the schedule.[1] Because of the volume of consumption of

[1] Many tobacco and whiskey manufacturers and merchants are said to

tobacco in our country, a comparatively low tax makes possible a government revenue as large as, and in most cases larger than, in most European countries where the tax rate is usually higher.

have gotten rich during the Civil War, at the government's expense, by increasing their output in anticipation of an increase in the tax rate.

CHAPTER VIII

SUMMARY AND CONCLUSION

To weave together the threads of a treatise that embraces the development of an industry through three centuries of change is no easy task. The diversity of the material and the variety of problems do not admit of a complete synthesis. The most that we can do is to note briefly some of the significant phases in the progress of the industry—in agriculture, manufacture, the labor problem, distribution, and consumption.

§ 1. *Agriculture.*—The cultivation of tobacco for gain has been extended from the narrow limits of the earliest Virginia settlement at Jamestown to more than forty states in the Union. For ten states it ranks to-day among their principal commercial crops. With the exhaustion of the soil from excessive use, the destruction of agricultural capital during the Civil War, and the opening up of virgin soil in the middle west and south, the center of leaf tobacco production shifted from Virginia and Maryland to Kentucky, Tennessee, Ohio and North Carolina. With the development of the cigar industry, the production of cigar leaf, protected by a high tariff since the Civil War, has expanded enormously in Ohio, Connecticut, Wisconsin, Pennsylvania, New York, and Florida.

The primary difference in the chemical composition of the soil of the South and the North has made their leaf tobacco non-competitive products; the Northern leaf is used almost exclusively in the manufacture of cigars, while the Southern leaf, with the exception of Florida tobacco, is destined for all tobacco products other than cigars. The vast area of fertile soil has enabled America to maintain its hold on the world market in the supply of leaf used in "manufactured tobacco."

For over two hundred years the development of the Southern tobacco production was bound up with the institution of slavery and the plantation system of cultivation. With the collapse of slavery and the destruction of agricultural capital during the Civil War, came a disintegration of the large estates and an ever increasing number of small farms. The inability of the large land owners to command an adequate supply of labor has made necessary the leasing out of small holdings to poor tenants under the crop-sharing system. The latter has supplanted the plantation system.

Simultaneously with the rise of small holdings, intensive cultivation was being hastened by the introduction of more scientific methods of cultivation. For since the Civil War a more extensive application has been made of the rotation of crops, commercial fertilizers, and improved methods of "curing" tobacco. Moreover, this intensive cultivation has been partly engendered by the growing demand of consumers for a better quality of tobacco. With the movement toward small holdings, intensive cultivation, and the emphasis on quality, the need in the South is not for land but for more labor and capital.

The problems of the planter are many: regulation of the crop, so as to avoid over-production as well as under-production; the inadequacy of the labor supply, especially in the South; the capricious forces of nature to which tobacco is very sensitive. The one problem, however, that has overshadowed all in the last ten years, and which to-day is more ominous than ever, is the Trust. By its strategic power as a buyer it has been able to depress prices on all tobacco except the cigar leaf. The demand for the latter is still largely from the independent manufacturer and not the Trust. Over seventy-five per cent of the entire Southern supply is purchased by the Trust and the "Régie" agents. With the power of the buyers concentrated in a few hands and the great number of sellers poorly organized and competing among themselves, prices are naturally low. United efforts and attacks of the growers upon the Trust have thus far been futile, and the problem is still as acute as ever. In their despair the Southern growers are looking anxiously to the government for a remedy or a mitigation of the Trust evil.

§ 2. *Manufacture.*—In manufacture, also, the industry has undergone momentous changes. Differences in the technical processes of production distinguish the manufacture of plug, chewing, smoking tobacco, snuff and cigarettes from the manufacture of cigars. As the former were more easily adapted to machine production, it was there that the domestic system was first displaced by large-scale factory production, and there also that the Trust arose and perfected its organization. The importance of machinery and large fund of circulating capital early led to a concentration of production of "manufactured tobacco," long before the Trust had entered the field.

In the manufacture of cigars skilled hand-labor has remained to this day the most important factor, machinery and unskilled labor having been introduced only in the production of the very cheapest cigars. This has prolonged the life of small-shop domestic production.

The large factory, however, is beginning to supplant the small producer. The advantages on the side of the former in the sale of the goods as well as in the purchasing of the raw material, are thus far the only decisive factors. The small producer has profited by the disorganized character of the retail market. The personal element, in the sale of goods, has been capitalized by the small producer, and this explains in part the slow headway made in the cigar industry by the Trust.

The Trust first appeared, in 1890, in the cigarette industry where concentration and machine production had reached the highest point of development. The immediate cause of the Trust organization was the endeavor of the large producers to escape from the intense and ruinous competition which resulted from the invention and introduction of new cigarette machines. The conditions which favored the extension of the Trust activities from the cigarette industry to other branches of the trade were: first, a disorganized wholesale and retail market which occasioned too high profits; wasteful competition among the host of manufacturers in attempting to create markets for their brands; and intense competition among the manufacturers in the purchase of raw material.

The success of the Trust has been due, however, not to superior economy in production and distribution, which the temporary condition of the industry made possible, but to the practice of destructive methods of competition. The principal weapon of the Tobacco Trust, and one employed so effectively by the Standard Oil Company, is local competition—underselling a competitor in a restricted field, while sustaining prices elsewhere. Temporary losses suffered in such competitive struggles are compensated for either by increasing prices to the consumer or by reducing the profits of the jobber and retailer after the market is controlled by the Trust.

The Trust first achieved success in the manufacture and sale of cigarettes, then in smoking and chewing tobacco, and finally in snuff and stogies. The cigar industry has alone remained to this day for the most part in the hands of independents. But even here the Trust is making headway through the organization of its retail agencies, the United Cigar Stores. The success of the latter means the extinction of the independent retailer, and with his extinction the markets will be closed to the independent manufacturers. From present indications it would not be too rash to predict the absorption of the cigar industry by the Trust quite as completely as the other branches have been absorbed.

§ 3. *The Labor Problem.*—The two forces that have revolutionized the organization of the the tobacco industry, namely, the introduction of machinery and concentration of ownership of the means of production, have reacted detrimentally upon the condition of labor in the tobacco industry. The introduction of machinery has meant initially for the skilled worker a reduction of wages and ultimately his displacement by a less skilled and a lower paid grade of labor. From a social standpoint it has involved the production of goods by a less intelligent and less skilled grade of labor.

Since effective organization among the laborers is rendered more difficult because of the influx of women and unskilled male labor, made possible by the introduction of machinery, the possibility of securing better conditions from their employers is thereby minimized.

Concentration of ownership and control by the Trust has tended to place the laborers at a disadvantage in bargaining collectively with employers. The Trust has not only exercised its privilege in refusing to recognize the Union of Tobacco Workers, but has taken advantage of the disorganized condition of labor by refusing to bargain collectively with its employees.

These conditions are especially applicable to the tobacco workers, where machinery has introduced a low grade of labor, women and children, and where the Trust has been most successful in controlling the industry. Wages of the tobacco workers are therefore very low.

Conditions in the cigar trade are more favorable. On the one hand the existence of a skilled body of workers makes possible a strong and efficient labor union which can insist upon fair terms through collective bargaining. On the other hand, skill is so important that the supply of labor cannot be easily replaced in time of strike. Moreover, in the absence of a complete control of the industry by the Trust, the terms of the labor contract are apt to be in favor of the laborers since the latter are very efficiently organized.

To no small degree has the welfare of the cigarmakers been protected by their powerful organization—the Cigar Makers International Union. In strengthening its internal organization this Union has made splendid use of a system of "benefits" for the protection of its members when on strike, unemployed, or in need of traveling expenses. In its contest with non-union manufacturers it has utilized to the fullest extent the Union label.

§ 4. *Distribution.*—Concentration in production and control of the industry by the Trust have made possible a more systematic organization of the wholesale and retail markets. This is especially true when the Trust has been most successful, namely, in the sale of "manufactured tobacco." Here the profits of the middleman have been reduced to a minimum, and are consequently low compared with the rate of profits in the cigar industry. The elimination of the jobber and the reduction of the retailer's profits are the most tangible allurements to the Trust. Where the Trust is strongly organized and exercises most effective control, the problem of the jobber is: How to take advantage of the larger profits offered through the sale of independent goods without being denied the privilege of selling the goods made by the Trust? For the independent retailer the problem is: How to compete with such attractive and so efficient distributing agencies of the Trust as the United Cigar Store and the National Cigar Stand?

Consumption.—The rapid development undergone by the tobacco industry in the last half century has had for its basis the expansion of tobacco consumption, especially in our own country. Most remarkable in recent years has been the expansion of the consumption of cigars: due in part to the improved quality of cigar leaf, and in part to the increased purchasing power of the general consuming public. Because of the importance of skilled hand labor and the use of a superior grade of leaf in production, the cigar is still the most expensive form of tobacco consumption. The total annual expenditure for tobacco is $500,000,000, two-thirds of which is for cigars. Since the Civil War the rate of per capita consumption of all tobacco has increased over 200 per cent.

For the consumers, as such, the problem of the Trust is not yet a pressing one. Where the Trust control has been most thoroughly effected in the manufacture and sale of plug, cigarette, chewing, smoking tobacco and snuff—prices of the finished product have not been materially increased. For this two reasons may be assigned: first, there has always been enough actual and potential. competition from independents to prevent too high an increase in price by the Trust; second, because of the convenience of the traditional retail price, on the scale of five, a small increase in price is not always practicable. Moreover, because of the great importance of brands and the necessity of sustaining their quality, it is very dangerous to substitute an inferior grade of leaf in the finished product. The sudden loss of trade in the sale of Havana goods by the Trust is a case in point. It is because the Trust is still in a militant state and still fighting for complete monopoly that it has been unable to raise retail prices to the consumer. Bearing in mind, however, the bitter experiences of consumers of commodities whose sale has been completely monopolized by Trusts, it is to the interest of the tobacco consumer to prevent, if possible, a similar monopoly in the tobacco industry.

For the planter, the independent manufacturer, jobber and retailer, the laborer and the consumer, the vital problem to-day is: How to prevent a repetition of the pernicious methods of competition already practiced by the Trust and how to forestall the more disastrous effects that are certain to ensue upon the attainment of a complete monopoly. Above all, the method of local competition—underselling in a restricted market—must be prohibited if competition is to survive. Remembering, however, that there are certain distinctly social economies introduced and maintained by the Trust form of organization and which it would be folly to abandon, the problem from a social standpoint in the tobacco industry, as in other industries, is—How to keep alive competition without the wastes of competition? How to preserve the economies of large-scale production and distribution without entailing the evils of monopoly?

The history of the futile struggle of the voluntary associations among planters, independent manufacturers, jobbers, retailers and laborers, against the Trust, only confirms the general lesson learned from other industries that nothing short of a second Trust with an equally great capital fund can successfully cope with the Trust already in control of the market. But we have also learned that a competitive war between two such giants, besides being socially undesirable, usually culminates in an even greater Trust.

The interests within the industry must join with the public in looking to the government for a solution of the problem. The history of anti-Trust legislation teaches us at least one thing: that no effective control or regulation of Trusts can be expected from state legislatures. The power of the regulating body must be co-extensive with the field of activities of the organization it seeks to regulate, which, in the case of the Tobacco Trust, is national. Disregarding the alternative of a complete government ownership and operation of the industry, such as is now exercised successfully in Japan,[1] immediate and urgent reform calls for regulation of the Tobacco Trust by our Federal Government.

[1] *Cf.* "*A Short Account of the Tobacco Monopoly Law in Japan*," by Y. Sakatani, Vice-minister of Finace, 1905, pp. 7-9. The Japanese government, after a thorough investigation of the relative merits of private ownership as it exists in the United States and government ownership as it has existed in France for some time, decided to adopt the latter for her own country.